RENEWALS 458-4574
DATE DUE

GAYLORD			PRINTED IN U.S.A.

Level Playing Fields

LEVEL PLAYING FIELDS

HOW THE GROUNDSKEEPING

Murphy Brothers

SHAPED BASEBALL

PETER MORRIS

UNIVERSITY OF NEBRASKA PRESS   LINCOLN & LONDON

© 2007 by the Board of Regents of the University of Nebraska ¶ All rights reserved ¶ Manufactured in the United States of America ¶ ⊚ ¶ Library of Congress Cataloging-in-Publication Data ¶ Library of Congress Cataloging-in-Publication Data ¶ Morris, Peter, 1962– ¶ Level playing fields: how the groundskeeping Murphy brothers shaped baseball / Peter Morris. ¶ p. cm. ¶ Includes bibliographical references and index. ¶ ISBN-13: 978-0-8032-1110-0 (cloth: alk. paper) ¶ ISBN-10: 0-8032-1110-4 (cloth: alk. paper) ¶ 1. Baseball fields—History. 2. Baseball—History. 3. Baseball fields—United States—Maintenance and repair. 4. Baseball fields—Design and construction. I. Title. ¶ GV879.5.M67 2007 796.357′06′873—dc22 2006025561

Set in Minion and Tanglewood Tales by Bob Reitz.
Designed by R. W. Boeche.

To my sisters Corinne and Joy and my brother Douglas

Contents

Illustrations

following page 88

Acknowledgments

I have incurred many debts while writing this book, and it is my pleasure to be able to express my gratitude here. Dr. Gail Rowe, David
MacGregor, and Ron Haas generously read the entire manuscript, and
it benefited greatly from their insightful comments. Beverly Dunn was
also kind enough to read a draft and, as a descendant of the sister of
one of the Murphy brothers, was able to acquaint me with new details
about the family.

Richard Malatzky, Reed Howard, Bill Carle, Joe Simenic, Pete Cava,
Jay Sanford, and Bob Tholkes were the most cheerful of companions
on the pursuit that started this book, as they have been on many others. David Ball has deepened by understanding of numerous aspects
of baseball history, as have many members of the Society for American Baseball Research (SABR). The members whose insights are directly reflected in this work include Kevin Saldana, Norman Macht,
Peter Mancuso, Stew Thornley, Dean Thilgen, Charles Bevis, Jane
Finnan Dorward, Tom Shieber, Steve Steinberg, John Thorn, Stefan
Fatsis, Bruce Allardice, Bob McConnell, David Nemec, Jim Lannen,
R. J. Lesch, and Priscilla Astifan. Countless other SABR members have
shared their knowledge with me over the years, and the impossibility
of listing all of them does not make me any less grateful.

I'm also very grateful to Rob Taylor at the University of Nebraska
Press for believing in a book about so arcane a subject and skillfully
guiding it through to completion. Additional thanks go to Paul S.

Bodine for his expert copyediting and to all the staff of the University of Nebraska Press for their diligence in preparing, distributing, and marketing it. Many thanks as well to Pat Kelly and Tom Shieber of the Hall of Fame and to Steve Steinberg for their invaluable help in locating photos. Finally, I am very appreciative of all of the friends and family members who offered sympathetic ears, valuable counsel, and much needed encouragement.

Any shortcomings that remain despite all this help are solely my responsibility.

Introduction

The Dirt beneath the Fingernails

Baseball is sometimes said to be older than dirt. It is one of those metaphors that sounds silly on its face but that still resonates because it hints at a deeper truth. In this case, the deeper truth is that neither baseball nor dirt is quite complete without the other.

Dirt is now a rare sight in urban areas, and unless embellished by a baseball game it looks a bit forlorn, as though it somehow senses that someone might decide that a parking lot would go nicely in its place. Baseball without dirt is just as unthinkable. Though adults tend to forget this, children never do—especially when they discover that baseball is an activity that allows them to get dirt on their clothes and actually earn applause from their parents.

The action of baseball is shaped by its playing fields in ways that would be unthinkable in other major team sports. Football legislates that the "ground cannot cause a fumble," while basketball and hockey are played indoors under as uniform conditions as possible. By contrast, baseball is played on fields of varying sizes and dimensions and even on different playing surfaces. When those differences impinge upon the play, they are celebrated. Baseball lore abounds with tales of bad-hop singles and such topography-influenced events as home runs off the Pesky's Pole in Fenway Park or pitcher Stu Miller being blown off the mound at San Francisco's Candlestick Park. Efforts to minimize such eccentricities inspire no such reverence. "Cookie-cutter" is the most damning thing that can be said of a baseball stadium, and Dick Allen famously quipped, "If a cow can't eat it, I ain't playing on it." This apparently odd state of affairs reflects an important bond between the game of baseball and its playing fields. Although ballpark individuality has been reduced over the years, attempts to eliminate distinctive features entirely are liable to be met with a deep-seated hostility that is rooted in the game's history.

Early baseball was very much a celebration of man's triumph over nature. The amount of work that had to be done to clear a wilderness was backbreaking. To do so only for the purpose of using that land to play a child's game seemed ridiculous to many. That is why baseball— then as now—is generally appreciated most readily by those with a keen eye for symbolism. Those symbolic reminders of the game's agrarian roots were key to understanding the message behind all of the ostensibly unproductive labor that went into creating a ball field. It was a way of saying: It isn't easy, but as a society we're winning. We have attained the necessities for survival and have enough to spare that we can consecrate some of that carefully plowed dirt and make it into a ball field. Then we can all play on that field, an act symbolizing what we have won: leisure time. If that sounds familiar, it may be because it was essentially the plot of W. P. Kinsella's novel *Shoeless Joe*, which became the movie *Field of Dreams*. What made that work resonate so deeply was that its basic plot is also a very concise history of the early ball field.

In turn, the history of the ball field is intimately connected with the history of the American people. Whether they sensed it or not, the men who carved out the first ball fields were replicating one of the central themes of the history of the United States. At the close of the eighteenth century, European settlers were scattered up and down America's east coast but had hardly at all ventured farther west. One important reason was fear of Indians and wild animals, and in some cases Spanish settlers, but an even more significant reason was the country's daunting geography.

A 1776 mapmaker ended his map at the Mississippi River and wrote off much of central Pennsylvania as "Endless Mountains."[1] He could hardly be faulted, as the obstacles to heading west were many and the rewards few. Many rivers had no bridges and had to be forded. Roads were primitive, if they existed at all. The western parts of Pennsylvania and New York were wilderness, while travel westward from the southern states was impeded by endless swamps.[2] The situation changed dramatically in the early nineteenth century. Lewis and Clark helped to show the way, and their would-be imitators were spurred by a series of developments and discoveries—the Louisiana Purchase, the Monroe Doctrine, the Cumberland Gap, the building of the Erie Canal and other waterways, and the emergence of the steamboat. Thousands followed their lead and caught "western fever," a phenomenon that further accelerated when gold was discovered in California. The struggle to forge the earliest ball fields was thus a metaphor for the pioneers who had trekked west in the first half of the century. Yet paradoxically, as we shall see, the building and maintenance of baseball diamonds eventually came to symbolize a very different strain of the American experience: the establishment of permanent settlements.

That paradox is rooted in a deeper paradox that is especially difficult to appreciate in twenty-first-century America. One of the greatest accomplishments of nineteenth-century Americans was the reshaping of their physical geography and topography. Yet those sorts of achievements are invariably unappreciated by later generations because either the process of modification has continued or the results are assumed to be natural traits. As a result, it may reasonably be asked what possible importance can be attached to the lives of two long-ago groundskeepers. And yet the question itself is the product of an era in which many of us have little direct contact with the land and therefore find it difficult to understand a period when the soil was so vital.

Throughout the nineteenth century and into the early twentieth century, the everyday lives of nearly all Americans were intimately connected to the land. Just as importantly, the economic and social structure of American life was based upon an inversion of the basis of European societies. In the old world, land was expensive and labor cheap, but in the new world, as George Washington observed in

1791, "the land . . . is, or has been cheap, but the most of the labor . . . is dear."[3] That inversion and its practical consequences necessitated a rethinking of all of the principles of life in early America. It is especially important to bear this in mind because it is no longer the case. Our dramatically changed perspective on land and labor today leads, all too often, to a sanitized and distorted view of America's earlier periods. As scholar Steven Stoll has observed, historians "have slighted the dirt under the fingernails of rural life even though practice and process were fundamental to writing about the countryside during the early nineteenth century."[4]

Though mainstream historians have begun to remedy this deficiency, baseball historians have continued to neglect what Stoll aptly terms "the mucky detail." As we shall see, that omission is especially unfortunate because mucky details about soil conditions have always played a vital role in determining the location of ballparks and even the viability of a ball club or league. This reality made groundskeepers essential to the success of clubs. These mucky details have also had direct effects on the practice and process of the game itself, by contributing to the origins of items as diverse as the pitching mound and the infield fly rule. Just as importantly, baseball's remarkable transformation into a spectator sport and a symbol that Americans could embrace as their national pastime occurred during a period in which Americans' connection to the soil was in crisis. The connections between baseball and the earth are thus deep and often far from obvious, yet well worth the effort to uncover.

Bat-and-ball games featuring many of the elements of baseball were popular among American children in the first half of the nineteenth century. The rules for these games were very flexible, enabling any number to play and the action to be abandoned at any point. The names applied to these games were equally flexible, with "base ball" (which was usually written as two words in the nineteenth century) only one of many appellations. Games had to be adaptable to thrive in a country in which land was cheap but labor and time were dear.

By the 1840s urbanization and industrialization were bringing the rhythms of life in the United States closer to those of the old world. Men such as the members of the Knickerbocker Club of New York City turned to baseball as a means of countering the unhealthy tendencies of city living. The Knickerbockers were principally a social club, but they took important steps toward elevating the sport into an adult activity by burdening it with standard rules, set numbers of players, and winning and losing sides. The late 1850s and 1860s, despite the interruption of the Civil War, saw the game's popularity grow exponentially. Young men all across the northeastern and midwestern United States caught "base ball fever," and the sport slowly began to make inroads into the South and West. In the process, the game was transformed from a gentleman's activity into one played by an increasing range of Americans, often for money.

During these years, a version known as the "New York game" outstripped the variants played in other regions to emerge as the "regulation" version of baseball. As Americans' favorite bat-and-ball sport, baseball also surpassed cricket, which had seemed a serious rival during the 1850s but was reduced to a niche sport by the 1870s. Many factors contributed to the ascendance of the "New York game," but land is one that should not be overlooked. Baseball had become the city game, and yet the land needed to play it properly was in increasingly short supply in the country's burgeoning metropolises. As a result, the bat-and-ball game that was most adaptable to land constraints would have the best chance of enduring. It is thus far from a coincidence that the triumphant version emerged in the city with the most limited land.

Neither cricket nor the "Massachusetts" version of baseball recognized the concept of foul territory, which meant that they required a much wider swathe of land on which to play.[5] As historian George B. Kirsch has noted, cricket's rules made it still harder to find an acceptable site: since the baseball pitcher did not bounce the ball to the batsman, as cricket bowlers did, "baseball diamonds did not have to be as well manicured as cricket surfaces."[6] This may seem a small point from a twenty-first-century vantage point, but Kirsch demonstrated its pivotal significance. The *New York Clipper* published a comparison of cricket and baseball in 1860 that emphasized that the latter benefited from the "trifling expense incurred in the preparation of a ground and the purchase of the materials of the game."[7] Similarly, a cricket club reported in 1867 that "with the difficulty of procuring suitable grounds, and the expense required in the necessary preparation, Cricketers must expect for some time to hold, numerically, a secondary place to those of the Base-ball persuasion, when almost any piece of ground with but little trouble can be made to serve their purpose."[8]

To create a suitable cricket field, it was necessary to locate land that was flat and unencumbered by obstacles in any direction. This was also true of other bat-and-ball games, though sometimes to a lesser extent. By contrast, baseball's concept of foul territory made it possible to deal with obstacles by simply placing them in foul territory. As we shall see, many early clubs made their homes at locales that were marginal for baseball and would have been unthinkable for cricket.

The new game afforded another way of making do with a poor field by appropriating the terms *infield* and *outfield* from Scottish farming practices. "Infield" referred to the land near the farmhouse that was kept fertilized and tilled, while "outfield" denoted the arable land farther from the farmhouse that was cropped but not tilled or fertilized. The adoption of these terms signified that baseball could be played on a field in which only a relatively small area was level and well maintained. Early baseball clubs often put considerable time into grading and sodding the infield, but generally regarded the outfield as an afterthought.

Just as important was George Washington's perception that America had inverted the old world's relationship between the value of time and availability of land. This meant that a ball game needed a faster pace than cricket to have any chance of success. As the *New York Clipper* observed in 1861: "Time, in this country, is money. We have not in America any class of the community who have the leisure to practice the game [of cricket] as they do in England. Here we can only devote hours where they can spend days; hence, we have to economise in everything, even in exercises required for health."[9] Yet the abundance of land—when it still existed—was also constrained by the shortage of time, since it took enormous quantities of human labor to make land suitable for ball-playing. Thus, the establishment of any bat-and-ball game in America was a daunting challenge.

This is the dilemma to which the Knickerbockers' version of baseball represented such a simple yet elegant solution. The combination of considering a foul a nonevent while also differentiating the outfield from the infield made baseball feasible on a wide range of terrains, while still making it desirable to have a large, flat, well-manicured tract. Simply put, these innovations gave baseball the flexibility that enabled it to become America's game. As Kirsch concluded, "While ethnic loyalties and tensions certainly influenced the fortunes of both cricket and baseball in America, far more important were the structural characteristics of each sport."[10]

Once baseball had outstripped cricket and other rivals and a standard version of its playing rules had emerged, the game began a more fitful transition to professionalism. The story of this extraordinary period of the game's development has been told often and from many different vantage points. And yet the feature of the sport's geography that must have been most singular to contemporaries has been largely ignored. Just as children who enter a ballpark are struck first by the dirt and the grass, so too mid-nineteenth-century Americans encountering baseball must have been powerfully struck by the use of valuable urban or arable land for so transient a purpose as a ball game.

That impression reflected the profound bond between the lives of nineteenth-century Americans and the soil. The financial aspect of this link was the most obvious one: agriculture dominated the nation's economy. There were many subtler ones, however, such as the Morrill Land-Grant College Act of 1862, which helped to make higher education both accessible and useful to a much wider range of Americans. Perhaps the deepest and most important one was that the American identity—throughout the nineteenth century and well into the twentieth—was intertwined with the idea of cultivating the soil. This was nicely articulated by a Missouri farmer who wrote to his future bride in 1911 that when a country "is made up of factories and large cities it soon becomes depressed and makes classes among people. Every farmer thinks he's as good as the President or perhaps a little bit better."[11] Just over three decades later, that farmer and his correspondent—Harry and Bess Truman—would become the president and First Lady. Aptly, when it came time to build Harry Truman's presidential library in Independence, Missouri, the former president's brother selected a low-lying, swampy site because he saw "no reason to waste good land on 'any old dang library.'"[12]

One reason for this tendency to overlook the centrality of the soil in nineteenth-century American life is the assumption that that role was a constant, an unremarkable given. What, after all, is "older than dirt" or less prone to change? And yet nothing could be further from the truth. Soil is always subject to amendments and improvements that may be invisible to the naked eye yet have far-reaching consequences. Though not biologically alive, soil teems with microorganisms and reacts to changes in its environment in much the same way as a living entity. The condition of American soil was in rapid flux in the nineteenth century, and this transformed the country in innumerable ways. Baseball was not one of the most significant ones, but it was one of the most symbolic.

The geographic history of the United States has been marked by two revolutions, one of which its citizens have recognized and memorialized while the other they have often ignored. The first revolution was the taming of a vast wilderness by a nation of settlers, a pioneering theme that is the basis of the frontier mentality underlying a large part of the American identity. The second revolution, subtler and less romantic, was the effort made by Americans to adapt to the vanishing wilderness by modifying their self-image from a nation of adventurers to a people who value permanence and tradition. In each revolution, considerations of land and soil played a crucial role since, as Steven Stoll observes, "people are anchored in place only as securely as the ground they till."[13] That reality was coupled with the still more fundamental one that "soil is a bank account for fertility that farmers draw upon, and the balance is always low." In a recurring pattern, American farmers "spent the balance down" until they could barely subsist and within a generation moved on "to seek fresh acres elsewhere."[14] Thus, what is so often romanticized as the American frontier mentality was in reality frequently an issue of land management as much as character or ideology.

And yet these different factors can never be separated neatly. One of the founding principles of the United States was its founders' escape from countries like England in which land was so scarce a commodity that it necessitated a rigid class structure and the concept of primogeniture to determine who inherited land. Early Americans embraced the glorious freedom of knowing that land was always available, but they soon learned that that freedom came at great cost. By the early nineteenth century, prodigal land management had begun to take an enormous toll. In 1818, the Society of Virginia for Promoting Agriculture summed up the dire situation:

> A soil originally fertile, has been rarely improved; and has, in many places, been reduced to such a state of sterility as scarcely to compensate the expense of cultivation. Taking possession of an immense wilderness, covered with thick forest, our ancestors were compelled to employ immense labour in clearing it. For a long time their utmost industry scarcely enabled them to open a sufficient quantity of ground to furnish subsistence for their families. Continual cultivation was produced by necessity, and exhaustion was the unavoidable consequence. New lands invited and rewarded the labourer; and cutting down and wearing out, became habitual.[15]

Unfortunately, it is easier to recognize the need for such a fundamental change than to make it happen. Indeed, by the 1840s there was a massive exodus from long-settled areas of many seaboard states. A surveyor of South Carolina reported that "the country appears like the former residence of a people who have all gone away."[16] Another South

Carolinian asked: "What impoverishment, what ruin, what desolation has the spirit of emigration produced in South Carolina? . . . No one considers himself permanently settled. No one expects his children to live where he does, or cultivate the soil which he is improving."[17] Americans were increasingly moving not because they had the freedom to do so but because their land-killing methods of farming left them little choice. An aura of impermanence permeated American life. As Daniel J. Boorstin has observed, it was around this time that Americans introduced the first portable houses. Known as "balloon-frame houses," this innovation "arose as a solution to peculiar problems of the American upstart city."[18]

The canals that linked the country were another potent example. A Scottish engineer studied these waterways and reported in 1838 that they bore little resemblance to European canals: "One is struck with the temporary and apparently unfinished state of many of the American works, and is very apt, before inquiring into the subject, to impute to want of ability what turns out, on investigation, to be a judicious and ingenious arrangement to suit the circumstances of a new country, of which the climate is severe,—a country where stone is scarce and wood is plentiful, and where manual labor is very expensive."[19]

These new approaches to building houses and canals were ingenious ways of addressing difficult problems, and they helped to foster Americans' reputation for resourcefulness and inventiveness. But impermanence can also take a toll, and the era's greatest American writers detected the subtle ways in which the national mind-set was being affected. Ralph Waldo Emerson perceived a country "of short plans," with the result that "Our books are tents not pyramids." James Russell Lowell echoed the sentiment: "We snatch an education like a meal at a railroad-station . . . and pitch tents instead of building houses."[20]

The severity of this impending crisis had not been lost on the Founding Fathers either. The retirement of America's early presidents to lives as gentlemen farmers is usually sentimentalized as a retreat from the turmoil of public life. In fact, they were immersing themselves in one of the most important issues of the day and one that threatened their vision for the nation. James Madison went from the presidency to becoming head of the agricultural society of Albemarle County, Virginia, where he sought to halt farmers' emigration by lecturing on the evils of such "errors of husbandry" as "shallow ploughing" and the "neglect of manures." He identified shortsighted farming techniques as a direct threat to the stability of the society.[21] As early as 1791, George Washington, in the letter quoted from earlier, lamented: "The aim of the farmers in this country (if they can be called farmers) is, not to make the most they can from the land, which is, or has been cheap, but the most of the labor, which is dear; the consequence of which has been, much ground has been scratched over and none cultivated or improved as it ought to have been."[22]

To solve this dilemma, Americans had to make dramatic alterations and become more like the societies that their forefathers had fled by adopting methods of cultivation that stressed permanence. It was a necessary shift, but a difficult one because it cut to the heart of the American identity. Many Americans turned to nostalgia to resolve the conflicted feelings that resulted. Even as their daily labors and the structure of their society lurched toward those of Europe, Americans clung with greater tenacity to the symbols of the frontier. The most obvious manifestation of this is the American fascination with cowboys, the Wild West, and new frontiers, which only increased as these items themselves became scarce. A less recognized symbol of this vanishing way of life was the game of baseball, which, as Steven A. Riess has perceptively observed, was "transformed into a moral equivalent of the frontier."[23]

As urban landscapes expanded relentlessly, the incongruity of expansive green baseball fields in their midst evoked nostalgia for the days when the American frontier seemed limitless, and settlers could always dream that greener pastures lay ahead. Moreover, the lives of men like groundskeepers John and Tom Murphy, who spent their adult lives with dirt under their fingernails from maintaining these fields, came to embody the dilemma of a generation making the uneasy transition from pitching tents to building houses.

1. Invisible Men

It is easy to rhapsodize about the glories of a smooth and abundant playing field, yet quite another matter to create and maintain one. And those who attend to those "mucky details" have usually not felt inclined to write about the results of their labor. In many cases, they were simply too tired to do so. Just as important was their skepticism that the written word could do justice to their labors.

As early as the 1860s, the maintenance of baseball playing fields was being simplified by some of the labor-saving devices that had helped chase American farmers' sons to the city, such as mowing machines and rollers.[1] Nonetheless, the task of rolling and mowing a lawn remained very time consuming, and most machines did not cut very close to the ground. Leveling ground was a still more massive undertaking, although it was made somewhat easier when railroad tools such as railway irons became available. For these reasons, groundskeeping was a vocation that attracted the rugged individualist. Billy Houston was a former prizefighter who became one of the top groundskeepers of the 1880s. He changed jobs frequently and helped to ensure that his services remained in constant demand by having, as one sportswriter put it, "a mysterious method of procedure which he refuses to divulge to anybody."[2]

The essentials of infield maintenance were of course fairly evident. As a newspaper account later explained, the basic formula was as follows: "Cover with a foot of cinders, topping it with a 12-inch layer of black loam, and sow in grass."[3] But soil conditions varied not only from diamond to diamond but also from one part of a field to another, meaning that only an experienced hand could give the entire field appropriate care. In addition, there were very specific requirements for the catcher's position behind home plate and for the base paths. The game's action depended heavily on getting a true bounce when the ball landed in the catcher's vicinity. It was equally important to ensure that the base paths were hard enough to provide secure footing for base runners. In 1875, St. Louis manager Mase Graffen wrote to his Boston counterpart Harry Wright for advice on base paths, and Wright responded, "I doubt if I can assist you very much as it is a question that has bothered me considerably." But Wright did offer a detailed account of his experiments: "it must not be the common building sand, as that will not pack or keep firm. . . . We have tried common sand two or three times but had to remove it. I have used finely sifted ashes and found it to answer very well." Wright then went on to illustrate another practical reality by explaining, "There is a peculiar coarse red sand that is used here in the public parks on the walks, that would be just the thing for a ball field, but it is too expensive for us to use not having a lease of our own grounds."[4] This need to economize made it inevitable that ballparks would be treated, in Emerson's words, more like tents than pyramids.

But how to meet the requirement to treat different parts of the field differently? The burden fell on expert groundskeepers, like Billy Houston, who were forced into an enormous amount of labor, as this account relates:

> He uses three or four different kinds of earth, the top layer being black. He sifts all the earth he puts on the runways [base paths] in order that nothing may be left there that would injure a man in sliding to a base. Mixed in with the top layer of earth is a sort of fluffy weed, which Billy says imparts a springy quality to the runway. As a result of the work he has so far done the runways and spots where the

infielders stand are as near perfection as possible, being so level a ball will roll on them like a billiard table. By sprinkling the earth is kept at the proper consistency and the runways are kept so smooth and springy it seems possible for anybody to steal a base.[5]

The magnitude of the groundskeeper's task is reinforced by this 1893 description of the daily routine of Pittsburgh groundskeeper James Pridie:

> Every day the club is home the ground is rolled with five ton rollers, and the field is thoroughly sprinkled with water; then the ground-keeper goes over the entire infield with a rake and levels the ground, fills up all the ground, and every little defect is looked after. Then the ground is rolled again. After the work has all been attended to the pitcher and batter's box is chalked, then the base lines, the coachers' and the outside boundary lines are all lined with chalk. After every game the pitcher's and batter's boxes are covered over with large tarpaulins, in case it should rain before the next game, and to keep the ground from dew.[6]

Though tarpaulins were being used to cover these limited areas by the 1880s, the introduction of tarpaulins large enough to cover the rest of the infield remained in the future, a fact that added greatly to the burdens of the groundskeeper's position.

Nor did the groundskeeper's work end when the game started. Billy Houston watched the game with an eagle eye and "if a ball takes an erratic shoot after striking the ground Billy notes the spot, and remedies the defect at the earliest opportunity."[7] In addition, groundskeepers were often saddled with a wide variety of other responsibilities, including fire and safety inspections, security, and crowd control. Philadelphia groundskeeper George Heubel was dismissed after being held partly responsible for an 1894 fire.[8] After a 1903 bleacher collapse, Philadelphia groundskeepers testified that they regularly inspected the stands for rot. A typical example of the jack-of-all-trades was "Dutch" Oehler, groundskeeper for Cincinnati in the 1880s. Oehler was reported to be a "superintendent, catcher, short stop, and lawn mower" as well as a good carpenter, "as the carefully kept stands bear witness." Because he had been a strong amateur ballplayer, whenever a would-be pitcher showed up for a tryout Oehler would catch him and determine whether the manager should consider him.[9]

As if this weren't enough, many groundskeepers were saddled with a wide range of menial duties. Some were charged with retrieving foul balls, with a Decatur, Illinois, newspaper complaining in 1904 that "The Bloomington ground keeper must have been instructed to hold the good balls when fouled, as we always bat a soft, mushy ball."[10] A St. Louis groundskeeper was even assigned to spy on club owner Chris Von der Ahe and testified at one of his divorce trials.[11]

Yet another unfortunate reality of the groundskeeper's life was the one alluded to Harry Wright in 1875—that baseball clubs rarely had long-term homes. The fact that these clubs were still struggling to survive meant that many of them were tenants at sites intended for other purposes. Racetracks, for example, were commonly adapted for baseball. Baseball clubs were also the tenants of cricket clubs in many cities, despite the fact that their sport had far surpassed cricket in popularity. Other clubs used facilities built for ice-skating, and one club, as we shall see, rented space on a field designed for polo.

This impermeability rendered many baseball clubs second-class citizens in their own hometowns and created yet another source of headaches for groundskeepers. The Worcester (Massachusetts) Fairgrounds were regularly torn up by plowing matches, for example.[12] St. Louis owner Chris Von der Ahe grumbled in 1889 that the Kansas City park was used "for a shooting grounds, too, and it is all full of holes. Of course the home club is used to playing there and have an advantage in that respect over visiting teams."[13] Both of these were major league parks, so it is safe to assume that minor league and semipro clubs faced even more adverse conditions. Adding to the sense of impermanence was the fact that wooden grandstands burned down with discouraging regularity. Baseball's early groundskeepers must have had the disheartening sense that, figuratively and sometimes literally, they were building castles on ground made of sand.

Moreover, groundskeepers were taken for granted when they did their jobs well, but everyone noticed when problems arose. Rain, flooding, and poor drainage, as will be discussed in chapter 4, could cause postponements that might ruin a club. As soon as the weather permitted in the spring, the field had to be rushed into condition and the grass put in so that valuable practice time was not lost. This was particularly true before the mid-1880s when most clubs still held spring practices at their home parks. But even after spring training in warmer southern climes became customary, wet ball fields remained an issue. In 1914, for example, the *Chicago Tribune* reported: "the pro posed morning practice [of the Federal League Chicago Whales] was abandoned because men were working on the grounds to put them in better condition. The shower of the early morning left the diamond pretty soft, and [manager Joe] Tinker didn't want his athletes to tear up the new sod with their spiked shoes."[14]

A perfect example of how groundskeepers were routinely expected to do the impossible is Cincinnati's Pendleton Park. Because of the turmoil that followed the demise of the Players' League, Cincinnati's American Association team did not even beginning looking for a site until March 1891. They finally selected Pendleton Park on March 27, but the wet field made it impossible to have the grounds ready for opening day, forcing the schedule to be adjusted.[15] Once the field opened, many more problems soon became evident. The club shared the facility with the Cincinnati Gymnasium, and a cinder bicycle track running through the outfield left a "great trench in far left center."[16] Moreover, whenever it rained, the water accumulated behind second base, making it impossible for the second baseman to get to many balls in his territory.[17]

Before a game on June 7, groundskeeper Red McMichael informed manager Frank Bancroft that rain the night before would make it impossible to play. But Bancroft was expecting a big Sunday crowd and insisted that the game be played no matter what. Wagons of sawdust were brought in, and men were still putting it down right up until game time.[18] Finally, the Cincinnati club acknowledged the need for a complete renovation of the drainage system and relinquished some of its home games.[19] During the four-week road trip that resulted, there were optimistic reports that the new drainpipes had finally solved the flooding problem.[20] Unfortunately, when the players returned home, they found that the trenches that had been built to alleviate flooding at Pendleton Park created a new problem. One reporter suggested that visiting outfielders be provided with a map showing locations of "the under path ditch, and other ditches tributary to it. There is no other way of playing the field. [Outfielders Emmett] Seery, [Dick] Johnston and [Lefty] Marr each have one in their uniforms. Until a man gets the hang of the under path he is liable to get some hard falls."[21] Infielders were only slightly better off, with the ground in the vicinity of the shortstop's position being "nearly as rough as a freshly plowed field."[22]

Shortly after this, the club disbanded.

What kind of man would choose to enter a vocation with so many obstacles and so few rewards?

John and Tom Murphy's parents, Morris Murphy Sr. and Bridget Griffin, were born in Ireland and got married in the late 1840s, during the years when the Great Potato Famine was devastating their homeland. The newlyweds stuck it out longer than many, but around 1853, with their infant daughter Mary, they emigrated to British North America (now Canada), where the family soon swelled to include five more children: Patrick, John, Johanna, Morris, and Tom. The family is known to have been living in Toronto when John was born in 1856, and may have spent all twelve years there.[23]

Canada had been a very popular destination for Irish expatriates during the 1830s because of the availability of cheap transatlantic fares. The influx was especially large at the famine's height in 1847, but the number of newcomers far exceeded the opportunities. The 1850s and

1860s therefore saw an increasing percentage of Irish emigrants heading directly to the warmer climes of the United States, while many who had originally settled in Canada moved south of the border.[24] In 1865, the Murphys joined this trend and settled permanently in Indianapolis, where two more children, Michael and Bridget, were born.

The city directories show that the Murphys lived in a poor region of Indianapolis known as Irish Hill, which was located on the near south side by the railroad tracks and was primarily populated by Irish railway, canal, and road workers.[25] The Murphys moved frequently in their early years in Indianapolis but always within this nine-block area. They had little choice in the matter.

The first six presidents of the United States were all men who came from backgrounds of wealth and privilege. As a result, tremendous significance was attached to the 1828 election of Andrew Jackson, a self-made man and the son of Irish immigrants. Although the symbolism was of undeniable importance, what became known as Jacksonian democracy still provided representation to only a small portion of the populace. Historian Howard Zinn has noted that "Blacks, Indians, women, and foreigners were clearly outside the consensus. But also, white working people, in large numbers, declared themselves outside [by allying themselves with the radical labor movement]."[26] The feeling of being outsiders was especially prevalent among the waves of Irish emigrants who flocked to the United States after the potato famine. Large-scale Irish emigration to North America was not new, but its scope during this period was unprecedented and its nature also changed fundamentally.

The history of Ireland is inextricably and most unhappily linked to that of England. English ownership of a sizable portion of Ireland dates back to the twelfth century, and the proportion increased steadily. So did the animosity between the two countries, which was sealed when the reformation left England predominantly Protestant and Ireland overwhelmingly Catholic. As Cecil Woodham-Smith put it, "So completely is the history of the one country the reverse of the other that the very names which to an Englishman mean glory, victory and prosperity to an Irishman spell degradation, misery and ruin."[27] By 1700 the Irish owned only 14 percent of their native soil. The hostility and the poverty-stricken state of the Irish people worsened in the nineteenth century when English landlords forced Irish tenant farmers to switch from tilling the land to raising cattle. Around one million Irish came to the United States between 1815 and 1845, yet many of them believed that they would eventually return to their native land. Those who remained were comforted by the assurance that the potato would always sustain them, since a single acre could produce enough potatoes for a family to live on for a year.[28]

This changed when a fungus devastated the 1845 crop and those of the succeeding years. Mass starvation ensued, and millions of Irish fled their homeland. The prospect of a country where land was cheap and labor dear made the United States the most appealing destination, and an additional one-and-a-half million Irish emigrants were brought there on vessels with such high mortality rates that they were known as "coffin ships." The desperate men and women who survived the voyage brought with them a changed attitude toward their homeland: "What had earlier been viewed as banishment was now regarded as release."[29]

Their adopted home did not open its arms to the newcomers, however. America may have seemed like the land of opportunity to the Irish, but upon their arrival they encountered hostility and discrimination. Much of it focused on the Roman Catholic faith of most of the Irish, but it spilled over into other aspects as well.[30] Irish men looking for work were in some ways worse off than African American slaves. One Southern planter explained why he had hired Irishmen to drain a flooded area instead of using his own slaves: "It's dangerous work . . . and a negro's life is too valuable to be risked at it. If a Negro dies, it's a considerable loss, you know."[31] Mike Walsh, one of the first prominent Irish American politicians, claimed that "The only difference between the negro slave of the South and the white wage slave of the North is that the one has a master without asking for him, and the other has to beg for the privilege of becoming a slave."[32] Even W. E. B. DuBois acknowledged that when he was growing up in Massachusetts in the late nineteenth century, "the racial angle was more clearly defined against the Irish than against me."[33]

Irish women were no better off. Many of them found work as maids, where their employers bossed them around so incessantly and made them work so many hours that they felt like "prisoners."[34] Yet these unfortunate women had to count their blessings when they looked in the newspapers for other positions and saw ad after ad that bluntly stated, "Irish need not apply."

There was one consolation for the exiles from Ireland. As white-skinned immigrants from an English-speaking country, the Irish had access to the ultimate leveler—the vote. The Know-Nothing party and other nativist groups tried to snuff even this hope by advocating stricter naturalization and suffrage laws and working to prevent Catholics from holding public offices. The prejudice was reinforced by textbooks that informed schoolchildren that the Irish were "quick of apprehension, active, brave and hospitable; but passionate, ignorant, vain, and superstitious."[35] Yet through all this, the Irish persevered, buoyed by the knowledge that having the vote meant that no matter how many hardships they encountered, things could be different for their children.

The Indianapolis city directory listings also hint at another thread that permeated the Murphys' lives. The children of Morris and Bridget Murphy were part of a generation of American men with outdoor skills who were making the uneasy transition to city living in unprecedented numbers. The years leading up to the Civil War had been hard on the independent farmer, as they had to adjust to competitors who relied upon mechanization and large-scale production methods. This increased emphasis on mechanization and the additional expenses of clearing and fencing land made starting a farm an expensive proposition beyond the means of most immigrants. Moreover, by the mid-nineteenth century Ireland possessed a peculiar mix of rural and urban characteristics. Though the country was slow to industrialize, it was also densely populated—most farms had been subdivided so many times that they combined the crowded feel of the city with the countryside's lack of conveniences.[36] As a result, most of Ireland's exiles gravitated to American cities, where they became trapped in the poverty and unhygienic conditions of slum-like tenements (which were often still improvements over conditions in their homeland).

America had long been synonymous with the idea of a limitless supply of available land, but that was never a practical reality for most Irish immigrants. What the Irish did have, however, was an understanding of how to make do in cramped quarters. That became a valuable skill as the end of the nineteenth century approached, and all Americans had to recognize that the days when farmland seemed infinite were coming to an end.

In 1891, the United States census bureau officially declared that the frontier no longer existed. Historian Frederick Jackson Turner pointed this fact out and sent shock waves across a country that had taken the availability of land for granted. Many Americans felt that their very identity was being threatened. Later historians have correctly revised some of Turner's assessments.[37] But his point really dealt more with attitudes than with latitudes, which is why it resonated with Americans. Turner quoted a "suggestive" passage from an 1833 guide to the west that explained that to the pioneer, "It is quite immaterial whether he ever becomes the owner of the soil. He is the occupant for the time being, pays no rent, and feels as independent as the 'lord of the manor.'"[38]

By the 1890s, fewer and fewer Americans were actually living that way, yet the underlying mentality was still prevalent. Turner's message brought home to Americans the distressing reality that they no longer had the "gate of escape" represented by the frontier—that the America of their imaginations no longer existed (if indeed it ever had).[39] And this touched a nerve. It did so, not because what Turner perceived was really new, but because he had pointed out a trend that had been strengthening for decades and that Americans had done their best to ignore.

Fueled by the wasteful land management practices long common on American farms, since the 1850s a steadily rising number of farmers had been faced with the sad necessity of sending their sons to the cities to earn a living. By coincidence—or maybe not so coincidentally—the total value of the country's manufactured goods exceeded that of agricultural products for the first time one year before the census bureau's declaration.[40] But only after Turner's pronouncement did it finally sink in that the cities had become the new American frontier.

As the children of farmers and other small-town craft workers moved to the burgeoning urban areas, they were disconcerted to find that most jobs involved working indoors and repeating the same tasks over and over instead of having the satisfaction of seeing their handiwork through the entire process of production. The tempo of their workdays also changed in response to the new demands for efficiency and greater productivity. Men who had been skilled users of tools were now operators, or even tenders, of machines.

The American West may never have been as glamorous as it was portrayed, but at least it lent itself to such myth-making. The industrialized cities were sorely lacking in this poetic potential. In the early nineteenth century, some had bravely hoped that American cities would become artisan republics in which all workers would be united by pride in their craftsmanship. But these dreams succumbed to the Industrial Revolution.[41] No one has ever found a way to mythologize factory work.

As the century progressed, newcomers to the cities increasingly found that, instead of working for a close relative, they were employed by a stranger, who they might not even meet. The result was that men "struggled to adjust to the new environment. The rural mind . . . was abruptly confronted with the phenomenon of urban life for which it was ill prepared. The recent emigrants from small towns often felt isolated and bewildered, as if cast adrift in a strange world."[42] Opportunities for first-generation Irish immigrants were especially limited. As late as 1885, a census of Irish-born Bostonians revealed only 4 teachers, 13 lawyers, and 1 dentist, as compared to 5,679 laborers.[43] Yet at the same time the Irish were far better prepared to adapt to and seize the cities' new opportunities than were those arriving from rural America. In sharp contrast to the bewilderment of the displaced children of American farmers, refugees from overcrowded Ireland found the overcrowded American cities familiar.

The building of the nation's canals was one of the opportunities the Irish seized upon. The first great wave of Irish settlers arrived in Indianapolis in the late 1830s to work on the Central Canal.[44] By 1863, two years before the Murphys' arrival, the burgeoning Irish populace had rejoiced in the election of Indianapolis's first Irish mayor, John Caven. Caven and another Irishman, David MacAulay, served as mayor of the city for sixteen of the next eighteen years.[45] The presence of one of their own had symbolic importance for the city's less prominent Irish residents, and it also had more tangible benefits.

Most of Morris and Bridget Murphy's sons worked as firemen, a profession that had become a mainstay for the children of the refugees from Ireland's Great Potato Famine. Historian Ronald Takaki has noted that Irish Americans made a concerted effort to vote as a bloc in order to create "Green Power." Caven and MacAulay were Republicans, but by the late nineteenth century the Irish had switched to the Democratic Party, and their solidarity enabled them to take control of municipal politics in most northern cities. This in turn meant that Irish names began to swell municipal payrolls, especially as policemen and firemen.[46]

"Laborer" remained the most common vocation of the Irish, and all of the Murphy men were also listed at one time or another as laborers.[47] But the term *laborer* is a very broad one. Many laborers did backbreaking chores that provided merely the prospect of putting food on their families' tables for as long as the work lasted. Yet this type of work also brought opportunities, especially as a result of the first stirrings of the parks movement in the 1850s. More than three-quarters of the workforce who created New York's Central Park, for example, were Irishmen.[48] For most of them it was simply a source of steady income, but the parks movement increasingly put a premium on a knack for cultivating the soil. As a result, opportunities for craftsmanship in landscaping were increasing even while traditional crafts were headed in the opposite direction. As the parks movement caught on in other cities it ensured that men with these skills were always in demand.

The evidence concerning whether the Murphys received any formal training or apprenticeship as landscape gardeners is contradictory. The *Washington Post* later claimed: "John Murphy is an expert landscape gardener, having followed that business since his childhood."[49] On the other hand, sportswriter Sam Crane stated that Murphy "is a natural landscape gardner [sic], and if he had been educated in the art he would possibly have made a bigger reputation than he now enjoys."[50] Whether any of the Murphys were formally apprenticed as landscape gardeners probably doesn't matter, since the field was developing rapidly. In particular, there was no blueprint for the application—baseball groundskeeping—that the Murphy brothers found for their expertise. It is, however, important to note that Irish immigrants' experience in building America's canals made them authorities on issues of drainage and irrigation, and the Murphy brothers' careers make it clear that this knowledge was passed on to them.

By the mid-1880s, two of the Murphy boys, Patrick and John, had discovered a new way of earning their livings outdoors by pursuing careers in baseball. The establishment of baseball as a successful commercial enterprise in this decade paralleled the coming of age of a generation of young men whose parents had emigrated from Ireland. These second-generation Irish Americans still found many doors closed to them, so many turned to baseball because of its promise to reward skill. In 1896, the *Washington Post* pronounced that "the majority of major Leaguers are of Irish-American extraction," a trend that led Jerrold Casway to term the last two decades of the nineteenth century the "Emerald Age of Baseball."[51]

Access to baseball for Irishmen was not without obstacles. After the 1872 season, Jim O'Rourke was offered a contract with the celebrated Red Stockings of Boston, but manager Harry Wright insisted on one condition: "O'Rourke can have the job if he will drop the 'O' from his name, as the public in Boston will not stand for the Irish." O'Rourke adamantly refused to do so, and Wright signed him anyway.[52] He became the toast of Boston as he led the club to five pennants in the next six seasons, en route to a Hall of Fame career. More importantly, he signaled to second-generation Irish Americans that baseball held opportunities for them.

2. The Pursuit of Pleasures under Difficulties

Baseball history starts with the Knickerbocker Club of New York City in the early 1840s. Though its members were not the first to form a baseball club, they were the first to create and preserve a significant written record of their rules and activities. At a time when literacy was being stressed and written modes of communication were replacing oral ones, this concern with legacy signaled a new seriousness toward what had previously been a child's game. So too did the club's high standards of conduct and the middle-class or higher socioeconomic status of its members.[1] Yet the club that brought a new level of dignity to baseball first had to overcome many difficulties.

Early Knickerbocker member Duncan Curry later recalled that in the club's early years, "it had been our habit to casually assemble on a plot of ground that is now known as Twenty-seventh street and Fourth avenue, where the Harlem Railroad Depot afterward stood." But in a symbolic moment, "the march of improvement [drove] us farther north and we located on a piece of property on the slope of Murray Hill, between the railroad cut and Third avenue."[2] As early as the 1840s, suitable urban settings for baseball diamonds were becoming hard to find.

Historian Harold Peterson has noted that the Knickerbockers were soon obliged to relocate once more, with the New York and Harlem Rail Road again forcing the move. The railroad coveted the same level ground that baseball clubs required, and they chose the Knickerbockers' new field for a subdepot and a stable for their horse–cars (railway cars drawn by horses). As Peterson observed, "it was beginning to look as if the club was going to have to lay out a different field every year."[3] It is small wonder that the Knickerbockers adopted the concept of foul territory!

The Knickerbockers eventually made the decision to move out of New York altogether, to a picturesque strip of land in Hoboken, New Jersey, surrounded by woods and overlooking the Hudson River. Its very name—the Elysian Fields—conjured up images of escape from the crowded city to a scene of unsullied pastoral beauty. One early ballplayer later reinforced this perception by describing the Elysian Fields as "an opening in the 'forest primeval.' The open spot was a level, grass-covered plain, some two hundred yards across, and as deep, surrounded upon three sides by the typical eastern undergrowth and woods and on the east by the Hudson River. It was a perfect greensward almost the year around. Nature must have foreseen the needs of base ball, and designed the place especially for that purpose."[4]

But nature didn't really do anything of the sort! This account was written years after the fact and reflects the preference for symbolism that memory tends to cast on remembered reality. Hindsight can be particularly misleading when it causes actual obstacles to fade into the background. By contrast, "Doc" Adams, one of the founding members of the Knickerbocker club, was no sentimentalist. Interviewed in 1896, Adams succinctly summarized the club's activities as "the pursuit of pleasures under difficulties."[5]

The Elysian Fields had in fact been designed in the early 1820s with an entirely different intention by steamboat and railroad pioneer Col. John Cox Stevens. British writer Fanny Trollope visited the site in 1831 and reported, "A gentleman who possessed a handsome mansion and grounds there, also possessed the right of ferry, and to render this productive, he has restricted his pleasure grounds to a few beautiful acres."[6] She commented favorably upon the paths that had been carefully designed to "exhibit the scenery to advantage."[7] Though Stevens's plan had been for the Elysian Fields to attract an upper-class clientele, in fact, its visitors represented a more eclectic cross-section. Fanny Trollope thus discovered that saloons were also part of the grounds, denouncing them as "abominations." The saloons in turn attracted prostitutes and "idlers of every disposition and capacity."

During the 1830s, other recreational activities began to be featured.[8] The Elysian Fields became a tourist attraction—as much a precursor of Disneyland as a truly pastoral setting! This made them a fitting site for the Knickerbocker club, which became the first of many nineteenth-century baseball clubs to be tenants in a "natural" setting where the natural beauty had been carefully enhanced by skilled care. When that care wasn't sustained, the idyllic setting was quickly tarnished. There are accounts of games at the Elysian Fields in which unmowed grass impeded players.[9] Trees were another major encumbrance. When the Mutuals of New York and Atlantics of Brooklyn played a home-and-home series in 1861, the Mutuals' greater familiarity with the eccentricities of the Elysian Fields was cause for concern. Before the first game at Hoboken the *Brooklyn Eagle* observed, "One thought will annoy the Atlantics—the trees bordering the field in the rear of the fielders, into which place the Mutuals bat most of their balls, rendering it almost impossible to catch them, even on the bound. On the other side, the Atlantics have the same advantage, and if they are able, (which they no doubt are,) to send their balls 'into the trees,' *ala* Mutual, their opponents will be annoyed the same."[10]

Indeed, the home field advantage proved crucial. The Atlantics "sent the ball pretty well into the trees," but the Mutuals were more adept at doing so and won 23–18.[11] In the rematch on the Atlantics' more spacious field, the Brooklyn side won by a lopsided 52–27 margin. Nor was this the first time that the home team had benefited from their familiarity with the Elysian Fields. In a series against the Gothams in the mid-1850s, the Knickerbockers won all three games played there but lost two of three games on the Gothams' field (with one tie).[12]

The early history of baseball is replete with these sorts of symbolic reminders of the game's ties to the country's agricultural roots. One of the first baseball tournaments ever held was conducted at the 1865 Michigan State Agricultural Fair, and the sport was soon featured at state fairs and agricultural fairs in other states as well.[13] At the same time, there was an abundance of literal reminders that finding a suitable place to play baseball was no easy task since the fledgling game couldn't hope to retain any site that was coveted by an established enterprise. As a result, the mantra of early baseball clubs was often: location, location, location.

Baseball's first flourishing took place in the late 1850s, at about the same time that the parks movement was striving to ensure the retention of at least a remnant of nature in the hearts of America's burgeoning cities. The idea that these downtown parks might make an ideal home naturally occurred to early baseball clubs. At an 1857 meeting in New York City that led to the formation of the game's first national body, a committee of five men was appointed "to confer with the Central Park Commissioners in relation to a grant of public lands for base ball purposes."[14] The game, however, was already becoming too rambunctious for the increasingly congested city centers. Detroit's city square, the Campus Martius, for example, became the practice site for one of Michigan's first clubs, the Early Risers, in 1860. Unfortunately, they broke so many windows in the nearby Russell Hotel that they eventually began paying the proprietors a flat rate.[15] Similarly, the aldermen of Marshall, Michigan, considered a formal petition by the local baseball club to be allowed to play in Capitol Square in 1861.[16] In nearby Kalamazoo, the village council reluctantly allowed baseball clubs to use Bronson Park, but they were admonished, "Have a good time, boys, but don't hurt the trees!" When the players started to use harder baseballs, the game was banned from the park altogether.[17]

It became increasingly apparent that baseball just wasn't suited for downtown areas. As early as 1860, Henry Chadwick was recommending a 600-by-400-foot tract for a baseball field.[18] These requirements would expand in succeeding years so the sport could accommodate an increasing number of spectators. In addition, the removal of baseball diamonds to the outskirts of town meant it was a common sight for them to be, in Al Reach's words, "two-thirds surrounded by carriages and wagons."[19]

As early clubs outgrew public lands, they were forced to become tenants at sites set up for other activities, which meant that their landlords could and often did evict them on short notice. As had already happened in New York City to the Knickerbockers, baseball clubs in cities and even villages around the country found that they could not count on long stays in downtown locales. The situation in Jackson, Michigan, was a perfect illustration of the hazards of holding a desirable location. Leasing space from the Horse Breeders' Association, the Mutual club spent considerable time and effort to prepare the grounds, only to be suddenly evicted in the middle of the 1874 season. The club found a new field at the corner of Fourth and Franklin, and these grounds were soon being described as being "if anything preferable" to the previous location.[20] By the end of the 1880s, however, the new ballpark also "[gave] way to the city's western expansion."[21]

Clubs that set up parks on public land had no more security. Early baseball in Rochester, New York, was played at two prime locations, known as the Babbit tract and Brown Square. But the desirability of these sites made eviction inevitable, and before long "the Babbit tract had been divided into building lots and Brown Square planted with trees."[22] A similar disruption occurred in Boston in 1869. The *National Chronicle*, a Boston-based sporting paper, reported: "Ever since the game was first introduced into Boston the common has been the scene of nearly all of the important base ball contests in this vicinity, and now that the city fathers have let it 'go to grass,' the fraternity had nothing to do but to secure another place to play or else give up playing to any extent."[23]

No doubt the decision of the Boston city fathers was influenced by complaints from neighbors about the noise and property damage that commonly resulted from proximity to a ballpark.[24] But the ballplayers exacted revenge by running a "Red Ball" ticket in that December's elections consisting of candidates who pledged to "grant our youth some spot for recreation." Eight of the twelve men on the "Red Ball" slate were elected as aldermen, and baseball soon returned to the Common.[25]

In most cities, however, ballplayers had to set their sights elsewhere in their search for suitable accommodations. Some clubs opted for vacant lots, but even these were becoming increasingly hard to find in many cities. As early as 1867, Henry Chadwick was warning, "The rapid diminution of localities for playing ball in the metropolis and its suburbs, as well as in other cities of the Union, points out to the leading Clubs of the country the necessity of taking prompt measures to secure permanent ball grounds, or otherwise the mere absence of a field to play on will lead to the disbandment of hundreds of clubs."[26]

Joe Weiss, one of the founders of Detroit's Cass Club, later recalled that around 1870 one of the club's forerunners shared a lot with a photographer's car. Predictably, one of the players "never failed to drive the ball through the window of this car, upon which the photographer would appear and attempt to 'take us' in a literal sense, but generally without success, as we were good base runners."[27] Even an ideal situation in the downtown area brought no assurance of stability. Detroit's Recreation Park was built in 1879 on land leased to the city by the terms of Elisha Brush's will. When Detroit mayor W. G. Thompson became president of the city's new National League franchise in 1881, it appeared that Recreation Park would become a permanent home for baseball in Detroit, especially since Thompson was also Brush's son-in-law. But the club disbanded in 1888, and within a few years, "the property was becoming so valuable that the Brush estate plotted it off into lots."[28]

A similar series of events took place in Chicago. Early baseball clubs played at Dexter Park, but its isolated location hurt attendance.[29] In 1871, the Chicago City Council voted to let the White Stockings play downtown at Lake Front Park only to see the site ravaged later that year by the Great Chicago Fire. In 1877, the club was granted permission to situate a new diamond at Lake Front Park, and it remained there until 1884.[30] But the 1884 season brought ominous reports that "The Chicago baseball club may lose its grounds on Lake Front. The

Illinois Central railroad wants the grounds, and has offered the city $800,000 for them."[31] In vain, the ball club protested that it had just made "new arrangements and improvements costing thousands of dollars."[32] It was a particular hardship to have to vacate the heart of the city when rapid development meant that there was no longer any "such eligible site within three miles of the central part of the city."[33] The White Stockings were allowed to complete the season, but predictably had to find a new home for the 1885 campaign.

As a result of such urban infill, an increasing number of clubs moved to outlying areas, where they encountered a whole new range of problems. The unpredictable nature of urban sprawl was a double-edged sword. If the city limits extended toward the ballpark, then the baseball diamond would soon be appropriated for other uses. But if expansion headed in a different direction, then the ballpark became too isolated to attract spectators.

Many more pressing concerns also arose. The more natural the setting, the more likely it was that trees would hinder the players. A major 1866 tournament in Rockford, Illinois, was played on a field on which "There was a cluster of five trees around third base. The catcher was hemmed in by trees with the exception of a space about 30 by 50 feet. The umpire could not see a foul unless it was hit back of the plate or a few feet on either side of the base lines."[34] The outfield was also "badly disfigured, in a base ball point of view, by trees."[35] An outfielder on the 1867 University of Michigan baseball team cleared evergreens and elms from the club's playing field. Team captain Lester Goddard wrote a penitent letter to the school newspaper apologizing for the actions of "some one who had more in mind the interests of ball players, center fielders in particular, than the worth of the trees or the feelings of the authorities."[36]

Even if the trees had been chopped down, there was still no end of potential obstacles. An 1868 game in Buchanan, Michigan, for the championship of Berrien County was contested on "an old potato field, full of stumps and stones and about as uneven as ground could be."[37] At a match two years later across the state in Tecumseh, players had to adjust to grounds "filled up with shrubbery" and with high clover that "checked the speed of the 'hottest grounders.'"[38]

Since most mowing machines did not cut particularly close to the ground, clubs had to be satisfied when "the grass had been cropped as low as machinery could accomplish."[39] Nor was mowing done with regularity. Ballplayer-turned-sportswriter Tim Murnane recollected that in Middletown "the annual cutting of the grass was put off until late in July."[40] According to a longtime member of the Riverton Ball Club, the club played in Biddle's apple orchard during its early days, and donations "enabled us to occasionally have the grounds cut."[41] Naturally, there were recurring complaints about fields that were "covered with dried vegetation about six inches high" or were "all hummocks and covered with coarse grass 6 or 8 inches high."[42]

Out-of-the-way sites also meant that the baseball itself got lost with discouraging regularity. Baseballs represented a significant expense for early clubs; there was no question of abandoning one that was fouled out of play. One early player later recalled: "We used but one ball then, too, and when some strong batter would lose it, the whole gang, including the spectators, would set out to find it. Occasionally some scamp would run away with it, and then there would be all kinds of trouble."[43] It was not until 1877 that the rules required the home team to have a second ball on hand and searches for lost balls were limited to five minutes.[44]

Hunting for the ball was not always an option. Tim Murnane later recollected playing for the Mansfields of Middletown, Connecticut, in 1872 in a "cow pasture" that was situated "close to the State Asylum, and was about the only place that the club could secure in this hilly country." An additional disadvantage was that "The ball park was located on the side of a hill close to the banks of the Connecticut River, and many a ball went bounding over the backstop to splash into the picturesque stream, when baseballs were highly prized."[45]

The frequent proximity of ballparks to bodies of water meant that drainage was yet another recurrent issue. At the Rockford park mentioned earlier, the outfield was surrounded by "a deep gutter that drained a nearly quarter-mile track. Only Providence's protection kept more players from breaking legs in that trap."[46] But the alternatives to installing such provisions for rain were just as unpalatable, since many fields were rendered unfit for play for days by a single rainfall.

There often seemed to be no limit to the obstacles that might be encountered at a ballpark. At Hamilton Field in New Haven, home of the Yale Club, the catcher had to cope as best he could with a large pile of stones directly behind home plate.[47] Similarly, after clubs in Rochester, New York, had been driven out of the city center, they set up base in a location so wild that at least one game was interrupted by a flock of plovers.[48]

When fences were erected at early ballparks, the last thing that anyone had in mind was providing targets for home run hitters.[49] The primary function of fences was to make it possible to collect admission from spectators, but an important secondary function was keeping out stray animals. One early Canadian ballpark, for instance, was enclosed in order to keep cattle out.[50]

Once the game began to attract a significant number of spectators, finding an appropriate place for them became yet another impediment to play. With profits so marginal, it was considered more important to accommodate paying customers than the ballplayers. Pioneer manager Harry Wright thus advised that clubs situate the diamond on the west end of their lot whenever possible, explaining: "It is better to cater to the comfort of the spectators, and take chances now and then [that fielders will miss balls] 'because the sun shines in their eyes.'"[51] With sunglasses still in the future, this made life difficult enough for fielders. They often had still more direct obstacles in the form of onlookers who ringed the outfield or stood along the baselines whenever the limited seating capacities were exceeded. Indeed, with stadium security personnel frequently in short supply, it was not uncommon for spectators to try to get even closer to the action and impinge upon the play. As a result, a complicated series of rules were crafted to deal with "blocked balls," which was the term used when a ball in play was touched by a spectator. Nowadays such a ball would be pronounced dead, but such occurrences were far too common in the nineteenth century to halt the action on each instance.

While "blocked balls" dealt with human interference, the many natural encumbrances to play were handled by ground rules. Ground rules are still a part of baseball, but today they are more likely to pertain to such impediments as speakers suspended from the top of a domed stadium. (Many announcers refer to a ball that bounces over the fence as a "ground-rule double," but in fact this is a major league rule and has nothing to do with ground rules, which are unique to each stadium.) In early baseball, ground rules really were about the ground![52] The prevalence of trees in the field, for example, meant that specific rules had to be enacted to cover cases in which a ball ricocheted off a tree and was caught by a fielder.[53] Before an 1870 game in Calumet, in Michigan's Upper Peninsula, "a rule was made that balls batted into a certain potato patch in the right field should only count as one base."[54]

Ground rules often provided the home side with a distinct edge. A host club in Tecumseh, Michigan, decided before an 1871 game that "balls batted into an adjacent corn field should only carry the batter to his first base." This decision did not sit well with the visiting nine from Adrian, which had a hard-hitting club and viewed the ground rule as an unfair home field advantage.[55] As noted earlier, the trees that bordered the Elysian Fields in Hoboken similarly provided a large advantage to clubs accustomed to them.

But no problem was more common than uneven ground; the metaphor of a "level playing field" was much more than just a figure of speech in early baseball. In 1863, a Philadelphia newspaper described a game played at Princeton:

> No one but a topographical engineer could describe that ground. To get to first base you ran up a hill, ran down to second base, up to third base and home base. The right field played at the top of a hill, the center field at the bottom and the left field in a gully. To the Nassau players, who

had been accustomed to and had overcome the difficulties of fielding on such a ground, the irregularities were of no account, but the effect was terrible on the Philadelphians, while the weakening feeling of playing on empty stomachs also told heavily against them. The Athletics, however, always play a good uphill game, and this was decidedly up hill and down hill too.[56]

That same year, the aptly named Mountain Club of Altoona played its home games on the side of a hill. In addition to turning fielding into an ordeal, this arrangement made it necessary to hire "the tallest kind of umpire to watch the movements of the out fielders as fully as should be done." In describing the accommodations that had to be made, one observer echoed Daniel Adams's later comments: "Playing a match on it may be truly said to be the pursuit of base ball under difficulties."[57]

Pursuit was literally the name of the game at the Boston Common. Despite the fierce battle that was fought to play baseball there, finding an adequate site within it on which to compete was no easy matter. John Chapman recalled that even at the Common's best location, "The left-fielder had about the hardest position to field and he was compelled to chase the ball up a hill."[58] This makes it easy to understand why the space-demanding "Massachusetts game" was abandoned in favor of the New York version.

An 1886 account noted that the ball grounds in Lincoln, Nebraska, were situated on an old cornfield where "The ground is so undulating that a man who is tall can, if he is at the home plate, just see the outfielders' caps, and the outfield is notified of a hit over the infielders' heads by the blowing of a horn on the players' bench."[59] If that wasn't bad enough, an 1887 game in Le Sueur, Minnesota, was played on a field that was derisively described as "so nice and level that the third baseman could almost see the first baseman, by standing on the woodpile back of the grounds."[60] And the Irvington club of Irvington, New Jersey, used a field in the 1860s that was "so irregular that at times some of the outfielders would disappear into a miniature ditch."[61]

Even moving to rural locations and battling the elements there provided no guarantee that the old problem of eviction would not recur. In Winona, Minnesota, in 1876, the local club's landlord "didn't really like to tell the Clippers that they couldn't use his grounds again this season, so he threw out a gentle hint in the shape of a foot or so of barnyard fertilizer all over the grounds. The boys interpreted it correctly."[62]

Nothing makes one appreciate the love that nineteenth-century Americans had for the national pastime more than reading accounts of the labor that went into a baseball diamond to overcome topographical obstacles. Cap Anson spoke for many when he later boasted, "When it came to weeding a garden or hoeing a field of corn I was not to be relied upon, but at laying out a ball ground I was a whole team."[63]

The pride that clubs took in their playing fields is often best illustrated by the scorn that was heaped upon clubs that were inattentive to their home fields. Following a tournament in Marshall, Michigan, an Ann Arbor paper sniffed that the field was "unsuited for the purpose, it being a clearing full of stumps, weeds and manure, while the entire ground was an inclined plane from right to left."[64] Another Michigan newspaper wrote sarcastically in 1875 about the home field of the Medley Club of Portland: "With the exception of a few trifling defects, such as a circus ring in the center of the diamond, carelessly left there by Van Amburgh a few days ago; a series of hills and valleys, in the midst of which the ground is laid out, and a score or two of stumps and stone heaps in the out field, separated here and there by rail and board fences, the Medley's ground is probably one of the finest to be found in the whole State."[65]

Ridicule aside, the eccentricities of these playing surfaces had a dramatic effect on the game in myriad ways, now largely forgotten. *Chicago Tribune* sports editor T. Z. Cowles later recalled an 1870 game in Memphis that was played on so sharp an incline that any ball getting past an outfielder would "never stop rolling until the batter had rounded all the bases."[66] This naturally left the outfielders with limited options about where to position themselves. Field conditions were incorporated into the game's strategies in a variety of other ways. Until the 1865 season, a batter was out if a hit was caught on the first bound, which meant that fielders had to gauge the flatness of the land where the ball was likely to land and then decide whether to try to catch it or one-hop it. Opposition to the "bound rule" gradually mounted, influenced by the fact that better fields led to the perception that the rule rewarded childlike play.[67] But even after the elimination of the "bound rule" on fair balls, undulating fields continued to have an effect on strategy. The current practice of putting a speedy outfielder in center field and a strong-armed player in right field didn't exist in the nineteenth century because there were more practical considerations. For one thing, managers had to take account of where the sun posed the greatest difficulty and position the most reliable man there.[68] Similarly, Henry Chadwick noted that the "peculiar character of the ground" needed to be considered in positioning outfielders, explaining that at the Union Grounds in Brooklyn, "the services of the sharpest outfielder are required at right field" because the hills there were so difficult to negotiate.[69]

With grounds so uneven, an outfielder who kept his eye on the ball's flight would be very likely to stumble. This placed a premium on fielders' ability to gauge a ball's flight quickly and accurately. In 1883, a sportswriter commended Joe Hornung for possessing "the useful facility of being able at once to judge and get under a ball."[70]

All of these factors were considerations when deciding which outfielder would play which field; a club might shift them around depending on the grounds. It also created the potential for a significant home field advantage. During the 1870s, the Wolverine Club of Benton Harbor, Michigan, played on a field that was notorious for an incline known as Hunter's Hill. Outfielders had to decide whether to position themselves atop the hill and come running down for short hits or station themselves at the bottom and climb the hill when necessary. Naturally, playing this field was far easier for a player who was accustomed to the hill.[71]

A Providence newspaper similarly complained in 1880 that a game against Worcester was played on "a rough broken field, remarkable for its pits and mounds, perfect traps for the unacquainted. The infield was hobby, making it impossible for strangers to calculate anywhere near correctly for the bounds of the ball." As a result, visiting players repeatedly headed "the way they thought the ball would bound or roll, and found too late their calculations were wrongly made, and that the sphere was rolling far out into the field or else making caroms into acute angles."[72] Such criticisms led the Worcester team to borrow the city's four-horse roller to level the surface, after which the field was pronounced as good as any in the country.[73] Unfortunately, such assertions by hometown newspapers were about as common as boasts by restaurants that they serve the world's best coffee—and about as reliable! One letter-writer asked in exasperation in 1884: "Please let a poor, ignorant subscriber know where there is a base-ball park which is not 'without exception the finest base-ball grounds in the United States.'"[74] The tendency to exaggeration was particularly true in this instance, as Providence visited Worcester again the next month and lost the game when an outfielder fell over a hill while trying to catch a routine fly ball.[75]

As these examples suggest, the components of a home field advantage in early baseball were very different from today's game. Early spectators were discouraged from showing partisanship, which meant that hostile crowds were very rare. Visiting clubs often had the disadvantage of arduous trips, but that could be canceled out by the work that the home club had to put into preparing the field. An 1865 account, for example, explained: "the Monroe men were all tired out by their efforts in preparing the grounds for the match, and this with bad luck explains the extraordinary game of their antagonists."[76] Hometown umpires sometimes meant a large advantage, but this was not a constant. Far and away the biggest component of the home field advantage was familiarity with the field itself.

Clarence Deming, captain of the Yale baseball club in the early 1870s, later enumerated some of the potential advantages:

If a country club could secure a fairly level meadow for its play it was in high luck, and the local vagaries of the soil were no small factor in the result of match games. Thus a team wonted to the hard-packed dirt of the village green, and, by ground hits vanquishing visiting teams easily, found grief and rustic Waterloos when, visitors in turn, it faced foes on soft and irregular turf, with grass so lush that it is of record that the ball was sometimes lost inside the diamond, and a home run scored on the equivalent of a modern bunt. If the home field was bounded by a near fence, thicket, or stream, all the better for the home nine after it had learned the local hazards. These variations of the field made the game fantastic in its changes. Nor was the country editor in a New England town, which boasted for those days a good field, without genuine if caustic wit, when after an acrimonious victory won on the home grounds he closed his account with the words: "The visiting club labored under the difficulty of playing on a level field and in the presence of gentlemen."[77]

The condition of the soil was another key element that could dramatically affect play. This was especially true in the critical area behind the plate, since the "bound rule" continued to apply to foul balls and was not permanently abolished until the 1880s. An 1876 account, for example, noted: "The sand has been removed from the catcher's position and the place filled with a mixture of leached ashes and sand, making a good solid spot sufficiently large for all practical purposes."[78]

If a club was less vigilant in its maintenance of the soil, the catcher had to adjust accordingly. More than forty years after the fact, a player named Jim McTague recalled why he began playing close to the plate while catching for St. John's College in Minnesota in 1874. He explained that the area behind the plate was very sandy, making it almost impossible to catch a ball on the bound.[79] Most clubs accordingly gave special attention to "building up and sewering the catcher's position."[80]

Soil conditions also had a significant effect on infield play. Under the apt headline "The Boys Go to Greeley and Are Badly Beaten, But Redeem Themselves on Their Own Grounds," a Boulder, Colorado, newspaper offered this explanation of why the home team had been defeated at Greeley: "The soil is not hard enough to play on, it being so soft and sandy that it is almost impossible to catch a ball on the bound. The Boulders are used to a hard field, and played to a disadvantage in this respect."[81] Connie Mack described an additional factor that complicated the positioning of early infielders. Base paths were kept narrow and as hard as possible to give base runners secure footing even when it had rained recently. But this created a dilemma for the defense: "If an infielder played in front of this path a hard hit ball was apt to kill him, and if he played back of it the ball often hit the edge of it and bounced over his head to the outfield."[82]

Pebbles were yet another impediment. They could of course be the enemy of fielders by redirecting the course of a seemingly routine ground ball. Nineteenth-century infielder Jack Glasscock became known as "Pebbly Jack" for his incessant efforts to rid his area of pebbles. A more subtle but just as significant consequence of pebbles was that they discouraged aggressive base running. Slides were rare in early baseball, and one main reason was that the conditions of the field made them very hazardous. (The crude spikes worn by some players were another factor.)[83] When slides did begin to emerge in the early 1880s, they led to some severe injuries and calls to ban the practice.[84] Though major injuries grabbed most of the attention, nagging ones were much more common. Johnny Ward noted in 1888 that "Sliding for bases is one of the most prolific causes of wounds and bruises. The hip generally suffers most in this exercise. Many a player, when he gets to his base, misses a patch of skin as big as the palm of his hand, but he doesn't say anything about it."[85]

By the middle of the decade, the custom of sliding had caught on, and new variations such as the hook slide had begun to emerge. One reason for this, though by no means the only one, was that groundskeepers were paying renewed attention to the base paths, making it less painful to slide. At least one club tried to turn back the clock, however. Before an 1886 American Association game against St. Louis, the host Philadelphia club scattered pebbles near the bases to impede the visitors' notoriously aggressive base runners. The Brown Stockings responded by taking out brooms and sweeping the pebbles away.[86] Early base runners also were well advised not to round the bases as sharply as today's players do. Though straying from the base paths would have saved a small amount of distance, this benefit would have been more than offset by the risk of losing one's footing in the more treacherous turf.

Hitting approaches were also influenced by the condition of the playing field. In an 1866 letter to the *Chicago Times*, one rather rabid partisan blamed his favorite club's defeat on the severe incline of the grounds: "You may say that the latter objection had to be suffered by both clubs; but there is a difference in the batting of both; one bats almost universally 'ground balls,' whereas the other bats high balls. If the field be bad, those striking 'ground balls' are at a disadvantage, as the force of the stroke is lost as soon as the ball touches the ground."[87] Although sour grapes are detectable in these comments, the case of converting a ground ball into an out indisputably depended on the condition of the playing surface.

All of these considerations illustrate two fundamental realities about early baseball. First, clubs enjoyed enormous home field advantages by virtue of their familiarity with the eccentricities of their grounds, especially at the outset of a contest. A Minnesota newspaper was not exaggerating when its account of an 1876 game noted that the turning point came in the fifth inning when the visiting club "began to feel more acquainted with the grounds."[88]

Second, the ideal setting for baseball was not "an opening in the 'forest primeval,'" since such locations contained far too many obstacles. The game required a natural appearance but one that was actually the result of long hours of cultivation behind the scenes. Truer words were seldom spoken than "Doc" Adams's description of early baseball as "the pursuit of pleasures under difficulties."

Not every aspiring ballplayer possessed the innate athletic gifts required to take advantage of the opportunity the game represented. It turned out that Patrick Murphy's playing skills were in demand but that John's weren't. Fortunately, John Murphy had his landscaping skills to fall back on and soon established himself as a baseball groundskeeper, with Tom following in his footsteps. (According to one note, the other two brothers, Michael and Morris Jr., also had careers as groundskeepers, but no proof of this has been found.)

John Murphy mostly plied his trade at minor-league ballparks until the late 1890s, but his brother Tom ascended much more rapidly.

3. Inside Baseball

Tom Murphy's early groundskeeping stops are largely undocumented. Burt Solomon claimed that Tom discovered Hall of Fame pitcher Amos Rusie while serving as groundskeeper at Indianapolis in 1889, but provides no source.[1] Since Solomon failed to recognize that John and Tom were two different people, it is more likely that he was referring to John, who probably was the Indianapolis groundskeeper that year and who had professional playing experience. It is likely that Tom assisted his older brother on some of his early assignments, which added to the confusion over their identities.

Wherever Tom Murphy may have learned his craft, he learned it well, and by 1893 he was groundskeeper of the National League's Baltimore Orioles. He was fortunate to arrive at about the same time as a crew of combative players who turned around a moribund franchise. In 1892, the Orioles had finished twelfth in a twelve-team league, a woeful nine games behind the eleventh-place team. Partway through that disastrous season, Baltimore's managerial reins were handed over to Ned Hanlon. Hanlon strengthened his position by acquiring part ownership of the club and then began to effect a remarkable transformation. He swapped two journeymen for future Hall of Famers Dan Brouthers and Willie Keeler. Other savvy trades brought over Hughey Jennings and Joe Kelley, both also destined for the Hall of Fame. Perhaps the most important acquisition was a feisty Irish American teenager named John McGraw. McGraw barely weighed 110 pounds, but opponents underestimated him at their peril. He emerged as the exemplification of a club that rapidly gained a reputation for a willingness to try any trick to win a baseball game.

Tom Murphy proved to be the perfect accomplice for their aggressive style of play, which became known as "inside baseball."[2] In 1923, John McGraw was asked to define "inside baseball" and told a story of a game between the Giants and Baltimore. Hugh Jennings hit a ground ball to New York shortstop John Ward, who threw wildly to first base. The ball rolled through an open clubhouse door near the Baltimore dugout, and Tom Murphy promptly locked the door. Jennings scored the winning run while New York first baseman Roger Connor tried in vain to get inside.[3] The story nicely symbolizes both the Orioles' resourcefulness and the important role played by their groundskeeper. The club wanted Baltimore's Union Park to favor their brand of "inside baseball," so Tom Murphy deliberately subverted the idea of a groundskeeper's mission. In contrast to Billy Houston, who had aimed to make infields "so level a ball will roll on them like a billiard table," Murphy used his skill to achieve the opposite result.[4]

A generation earlier, setting aside land for a frivolous activity like baseball had been a symbol that Americans were winning their battle against the country's wildernesses. Tom Murphy's work at Union Park showed that Americans had taken the next logical step: skilled craftsmen like Murphy had so thoroughly mastered their natural surroundings that they were now able to shape it to any end they desired. John McGraw later recalled: "We got Murphy to mix the soil of the infield with a form of clay which, when wet and rolled, was almost as hard as concrete and gave us a 'fast track' to work on. We went even further in having Tom build up the third-base line from the outside so the bunt wouldn't roll foul. And I do believe Tom had the first-base line on a slight downgrade from home plate to help our running speed. I know it wasn't uphill."[5] Sportswriter Hugh Fullerton went further, observing that in order to provide an advantage to the Orioles, "the base lines were filled in with a cementlike substance, which was wetted down and tamped hard. The edges of the base lines were banked up like billiard cushions to keep bunts from rolling foul. . . . The runways were down hill to first base, down hill to second, up a steep grade to third, and down hill to home."[6]

The Orioles' hitters soon realized that the prevalence of clay in the dirt in front of the plate presented them with another opportunity. They perfected the art of hitting down on the ball so sharply that they could make it to first base before any infielder could make a play. This tactic was so closely associated with the Orioles that it earned the name it is still known by—the "Baltimore Chop." The *Baltimore News* observed in 1896 that

> The Baltimore Club has already originated several dis-
> tinctive plays which have made it famous and which have
> been copied with more or less success by others. Foremost
> among these are the "hit and run" tactics. Now a new style
> of hitting will be recorded in the base ball history of '96
> and credited to the Orioles. It is "chopping" the ball, and a
> chopped ball generally goes for a hit. It requires great skill
> in placing to work this trick successfully, and it is done in
> this fashion: A middle-height ball is picked out and is at-
> tacked with a terrific swing on the upper side. The ball is
> made to strike the ground from five to ten feet away from
> the batsman, and, striking the ground with force bounds
> high over the head of the third or first baseman. In nearly
> every game lately has this little teaser been successfully
> employed, and yesterday two such hits were made.[7]

Murphy kept the outfield uneven, with a hill in right field that Willie Keeler had mastered but that was "the terror of visiting players."[8] He deliberately kept the outfield grass thick and tangled, especially in right field. Hugh Fullerton explained: "The ground was sloping toward right field, where Keeler played, and right field always was ragged and full of weeds, rough spots, hollows, and hills. . . . Keeler had a lot of runways, like rabbit paths, that no one except himself knew, and he knew the angles of a throw when the ball rolled down the hill, out into foul ground, and into the deep gulley [sic] against the stand."[9]

Some alleged that the grass was kept long for a still more sinister purpose. Base hits by Baltimore players would naturally get lost in the grass and result in extra bases. But when the visiting team hit such a ball, the Orioles' outfielders found it easily, prompting whispers that there were extra balls hidden in the weeds.[10] A similarly dubious ploy was used to aid the pitchers. Pitchers of the era relied on the dirt around the pitching rubber to rub the ball down, so Murphy would sprinkle soap flakes near the rubber. Visiting pitchers would reach down and get a soapy mess. But the home pitchers, tipped off beforehand as to where the flakes were located, could find solid dirt.[11] Hugh Fullerton believed that the cumulative effect was to transform the park into "the most unfair grounds ever constructed." He maintained that "the grounds, adapted perfectly to the home team's style of play, did more to win pennants than anything else."[12]

Though to what degree Tom Murphy's work helped the Orioles may be debated, there is no disputing the club's amazing success during his tenure. Baltimore improved from twelfth to eighth in 1893 and then reeled off three consecutive pennants from 1894 to 1896 and reached five straight Temple Cups, a postseason playoff that featured the top two teams in the National League (which by then was the only major league). Moreover, the evidence strongly suggests that Murphy's handiwork was responsible for at least a few wins a year. Between 1894 and 1898, the Orioles boasted an excellent 188-141 won-loss record for a .571 percentage on the road. But at home, they were virtually unbeatable, with a 264-73 record that represents a .783 winning percentage. The difference between the two figures remains one of the largest home field advantages in baseball history, and it became proverbial that "There is not a stronger team in the league on its 'own ash heap' than Hanlon's warriors."[13]

At least as significant as the Orioles' skein of pennants is the legacy they left of how to play the game. In 1894, Johnny Ward of the Giants is said to have remarked: "This isn't baseball the Orioles are playing. It's a whole new game." Indeed, Americans were beginning to approach their games in a way that differed from that of other countries. Sociologist Reuel Denney referred to a specific rugby rule to illustrate a distinguishing characteristic of American athletes of the late nineteenth century. British athletes were able to quickly arrive at a workable interpretation of the ambiguously worded rule, which suggested that the strong British tradition that "good form" is what matters most in sports continued to hold sway. American athletes, in contrast, were more likely to produce irreconcilable interpretations of the ambiguous rule. To settle the ensuing disputes, "an effort was undertaken, at once systematic and gradual, to fill in by formal procedures the vacuum of etiquette and, in general, to adapt the game to its new cultural home."[14] This in turn helped create what Denney called "the paradoxical belief that competition is natural—but only if it is constantly re-created by artificial systems of social rules that direct energies into it."[15]

Something was certainly injecting the Orioles with competitive fervor. The extent to which the Orioles' style of play differed from earlier clubs is often exaggerated. Many of the elements of "inside baseball" with which they are now associated—cutting bases, interfering with base runners, violently upending fielders—were practiced earlier, and in some cases more extensively, by clubs like Chicago, St Louis, and Cleveland. But what did differentiate the Orioles was how forthright they were about their approach. Previous clubs, no matter how hard they tried to win, paid lip service to the gentlemanly customs established by the Knickerbockers. They continued to cloak their ambition in the accepted rhetoric in which baseball was a test of character, as manifested by such traits as discipline and teamwork. The Orioles abandoned such pretense, openly avowing that ethical considerations did not constrain them from trying to win baseball games. John Mc-Graw claimed that the question was not whether hiding an extra ball in the outfield grass was right, since "it was the best idea at the time."[16] He explained: "We never thought up such advantages on the basis of sportsmanship or lack of it. I had trained myself from the earliest days to think up little and big things that might be anticipated by the rule changers next year. With us, only the written rules counted, and if you could come up with something not covered by the rules, you were ahead of the slower-thinking opposition by at least a full season."[17]

In short, McGraw and his teammates had mastered what Reuel Denney called the "artificial system of social rules" known as the baseball rule book. By taking that work as their guide, while explicitly rejecting the abstract notions that had traditionally restrained competitiveness, the Orioles were creating what Ward aptly called a "whole new game." One symbol of the way in which the Orioles turned baseball on its head was an extraordinary transformation in the meaning of terms like *aggressive* and *hustling*. Previously, these terms had had negative connotations because they suggested an ungentlemanly desire to advance beyond one's station. But teams like the Orioles rejected such notions and adopted terms like *aggressiveness* and *hustling* as badges of merit. John McGraw would take this even further, saying, "Aggressiveness is the main thing in baseball."[18]

In vain, traditionalists like sportswriter Henry Chadwick complained that

> Too many scribes—one in particular—appear to regard "aggressiveness" and hustling as especially applicable to manly play in the field, whereas both are terms appropriate to the very reverse object. It is worth while to define these two terms as applied to base ball. Webster defines "hustling" as "shaking together, pushing and crowding." The base ball definition of the word as illustrated in the professional arena, is simply to endeavor to win a game either by fair means or foul. "Hustling" is, according to the base ball definition of the word, to yell like a mad bull on the coaching lines; to prevent a batsman or a fielder or base runner from making his point of play by irritating or balking him; by willfully colliding with him, or tripping him up by striking him on his arm to prevent his throwing accurately, by yelling at him when about to catch a

ball; in fact by any one of the means of prevention of playing his point known under the generic term of "dirty ball
playing."[19]

Chadwick was not merely fighting a losing battle but one that had
already been lost. His views reflected his own background as a member of a prominent English family. Baseball, however, was increasingly
being dominated by men who viewed America as a land of new opportunities and the game of baseball as the most accessible of those
opportunities.

The Irish in particular saw little reason to be deferential to author-
ity. Their experience for generations had been that laws were made by
the English to thwart their interests. As a result, the Irish tended to see
any means of circumventing rules as legitimate. Second-generation
Irishmen like John McGraw and the Murphys exemplified this aggressive, resourceful approach, a fact that did not escape comment in
an era when ethnic stereotypes were commonplace. In 1896, another
prominent Irish American, New York manager Bill Joyce, remarked:
"Take an Irishman and tell him what to do, and he is liable to give you
an argument. He has his own ideas. So I have figured it out this way.
Get an Irishman to do the scheming. Let him tell the Germans what
to do and then you will have a great combination."[20] A sportswriter
added in 1907, "Gameness, aggressiveness, baseball brains—the typical Irish ballplayer has all of these."[21] It is accordingly fitting that Mc-
Graw thought of Tom Murphy when asked to define "inside baseball."
For the groundskeeper's open manipulation of the last elements of
baseball that were not subject to ironclad rules was the most tangible
manifestation of the threat his team posed to baseball's traditional un-
derpinnings.

Success always breeds imitation, and the Orioles and their rule-
bending ways were no exception. McGraw later observed that "Players
in the old days never complained much about being victimized, so
long as they could square it the same way, or improve upon a trick."[22]
Few rival clubs were able to manipulate their fields as effectively as

Tom Murphy, but many tried and at least one club devised a new variation. In 1895, Charles Comiskey's St. Paul team had seven left-handed hitters, which enabled him to tailor his ballpark to suit them. A contemporary sporting paper noted that Comiskey had deliberately "adjusted his diamond so that the right foul line crosses the fence just a little beyond first base, nearly twenty-five feet nearer even than the close fence at the grounds back of the West. In order to make this arrangement some strange work had to be done in the rest of the field, the third base being almost within a traveling distance of the front of the bleacher, and the left foul line running almost parallel with the long fence. One-half of the grand stand, too, has to face the sun in order to accommodate Charley's eccentric batsmen."[23]

Though such brazen tactics produced winning baseball, they also alienated spectators. Baseball fans were accustomed to Henry Chadwick's insistence that the game was akin to a morality play in which the side with the best character traits triumphed. Some of them no doubt realized that that wasn't what always happened, but that didn't mean they were ready to accept clubs like the Orioles openly thumbing their noses at that cherished ideal. The handiwork of Tom Murphy was a still more direct challenge to this tradition, since every blade of grass proclaimed that the club's sole focus was on winning.

At the same time that unrestrained competitiveness was creating an unappealing brand of baseball, a not dissimilar phenomenon was taking place in the business world. Unrestrained capitalism was producing the "robber barons" who created trusts and combines, ruthlessly driving smaller competitors out of business. The American public grew increasingly wary of the trusts that took over such industries as oil, sugar, and railroads, but most people felt helpless to do anything because they could not part with such essential products. Baseball, however, was a luxury. When baseball ownership began to mimic the trusts, fans had a chance to express their disapproval of both overly competitive baseball and the anticompetitive trusts by staying away from ballparks. The result was that the nineteenth century ended with baseball in the depths of a serious crisis. Dire predictions of baseball's imminent demise were nothing new, of course. Indeed, the game had been regarded as a fad during it first great boom in 1866, and ever since there had been continual warnings that baseball was dying out.[24]

By the end of the century, such dire predictions had become such a recurrent feature that many ceased to take them seriously. One reporter aptly observed, "But a few short years ago it was no uncommon occurrence to find intelligent persons asking, and in the most serious way, 'What is going to take the place of baseball, now that the sport is dying out?' The interrogations came mostly from parties who had not followed the national game from the early seventies and therefore were not familiar with the phenix-like performances of the pastime in nearly every quarter of the United States."[25] And yet there were ominous signs that this latest crisis was more serious than previous ones. Earlier doomsayers had usually placed the blame on players who were too susceptible to the influence of money, drink, and game fixers. As grave as these problems were, complaints about them always carried the implicit message that the game could be saved by driving out the guilty parties. In the 1890s, however, for the first time the game's problems were associated with a source that was much harder to address. Although A. G. Spalding's comments on baseball's turn-of-the-cen tury travails were often self-serving, he was right on the money when he said that the trouble "was not with gamblers or with players, but with club officials, generally termed *magnates*, and it will be readily understood how difficult a matter it was to deal with them."[26]

The players had attempted their revolution in 1890 by forming the Players' League (a movement in which, as Jerrold Casway has noted, Irish ballplayers played a very prominent role).[27] When the circuit folded after one season, the National League owners pressed their advantage and maneuvered the American Association out of existence. From 1892 on, the National League owners had the monopoly that they had dreamed of: a single twelve-team "big league." It didn't work out as well as they had envisioned. The war with the Players' League had weakened the National League owners, and New York owner John B. Day had had to rely on financial support from the other magnates.

This established a precedent, and several other owners began to hold stock in more than one club. This dangerous course culminated in 1899 in a series of maneuvers by owners who controlled two clubs to cynically exploit that fact by trying to create one megateam and one also-ran. The most extreme result of "syndicate ownership" was the sorry sight of the Cleveland Spiders, a club that compiled a 20-134 record and played the second half of the season on the road because nobody in Cleveland wanted to watch them.

The owners also tried to recoup their losses by slashing player salaries. Some players responded with the only option they had left—retirement. Superstar pitcher Amos Rusie, who was said to have been discovered by Tom Murphy, walked away from the game for an entire year. Other stars such as Bill Lange, Johnny Ward, and Mike Griffin retired for good, though they were still at or near their primes. The Baltimore club, as will be discussed in chapter 6, was another casualty. Fans, deprived of star players and forced instead to watch hopeless teams like the Spiders, understandably became disenchanted. Baseball needed to reinvent itself to survive. The National League's unimaginative leadership showed no signs of the vision needed to make the necessary changes until the emergence of the rival American League in 1901 forced them to do so. This led to important adjustments in three areas—field conditions, umpiring, and ownership—during the first decade of the twentieth century. Though none of these changes was perfect, they were enough to restore public faith that baseball cared about fairness.

Baseball's rules had gradually been fine-tuned so that by the 1890s most of the loopholes by which a club could gain an advantage had been eliminated. But as Tom Murphy's stint with the Orioles had shown, the conditions of the playing field were one notable exception. The game responded in the early twentieth century with the first historic adjustment: extending the concept of fair play embodied in the rules to include the playing field. As chapters 12 and 13 will describe in greater detail, these changes ensured that there would henceforth be, both literally and figuratively, a level playing field. Christy Mathewson summed up the situation aptly in 1912: "The habit of doctoring grounds is not so much in vogue now as it once was. For a long time it was considered fair to arrange the home field to the best advantage of the team which owned it, for otherwise what was the use in being home? . . . But lately among the profession, sentiment and baseball legislation have prevailed against the doctoring of grounds, and it is done very little."[28]

The second adjustment was to make the lives of umpires a little easier. Umpires were, of course, already impartial in theory. In practice, however, they were almost always locals, with predictable results, until the late 1870s. In the early 1880s the major leagues adopted salaried crews of traveling umpires, but several factors continued to create at least the perception of an advantage for the home team. For one thing, the umpires were bullied and undercut at every turn, a problem that was exacerbated by the growing emphasis on aggressiveness. Umpires were the victims of rampant verbal abuse and occasionally even of physical abuse from players, managers, and fans. This led to the dangerous impression that they could be intimidated into favoritism by the home team and the crowd. Efforts by league owners to fire umpires who displeased them only made matters worse. As A. G. Spalding explained, "Umpires who did not give [these owners' clubs] the best of every close decision would be protested and changed. The telegraph wires were kept hot with messages from such magnates demanding that this umpire be sent here, and that umpire be sent there, and the other umpire be sent elsewhere, to meet the whims and caprices of these persistent mischief-makers."[29] Since most owners only attended home games, an umpire was under tremendous pressure to favor the home side. In addition, each game continued to be officiated by a lone umpire. Experiments had been made in the late 1880s with a second umpire, and the Players' League had used a two-umpire system during its single season in 1890. The National League, however, elected to continue using one umpire for most games.

This decision was particularly significant because the benefits of using the second umpire had been obvious, while the National League offered no compelling reason for clinging to one. Clubs like the Orioles took advantage by flagrantly cutting inside bases instead of touching them whenever the umpire's back was turned. Fans could hardly be blamed for concluding that the National League was more interested in profits than in fairness. Reporters drew the same conclusion, with one observing in 1897 that opposition to a second umpire was one point on which "the Little Five and the Big Seven [owners] heartily concur, as they do on every question where the wallet comes directly into play."[30] National League president Nick Young didn't help matters when he specifically instructed umpire John Kelly in 1888 to give the home team the benefit of the doubt. He explained that "To carry out this idea it is not necessary to be 'a home umpire,' but where an honest doubt exists the home club should not be the sufferer."[31] Undoubtedly, Young felt that this approach might alleviate the pressures on his beleaguered staff. If anything, it did the opposite, since it gave both sides all the more excuse to object to any close call. The home crowd would howl if it weren't given the benefit of the doubt on every close call, while the visitors would understandably protest if too many calls favored the home team. Henry Chadwick offered a poignant description of the umpire's resulting isolation: "The moment an umpire takes his position in a game he finds opposed to him at the very outset eighteen contesting players on the field. Then, too, among his special foes are the 'Hoodlums' of the bleachers, who go for him on principle; besides which there are his partisan enemies in the grand stand."[32]

Researcher John Schwartz has compiled detailed statistics on the number of umpires used by the two major leagues in the early twentieth century. Between 1901 and 1903, the ratio of umpires to games was 1.18, meaning that a single umpire was officiating in more than four games out of five. The number rose gradually over the next five years, but in 1908 it was still more common than not for an umpire to work alone. The 1909 season finally saw approximately four out of five games feature two umpires, and over the next two years the second official became standard practice.[33] Major league baseball had at last made a commitment to providing the extra pair of eyes it had long needed.

Baseball's third major adjustment crystallized after the 1901 season during a tug of war for control of the National League between A. G. Spalding and four owners led by New York's Andrew Freedman. These four magnates had concocted a plan by which syndicate ownership would be expanded into a full-fledged trust, with all eight owners having stock in the league as a whole. According to Spalding's highly self-serving account, "The special phase of aggressive onslaught against League interests that called me from an unofficial position, as simply an honorary member, into an active struggle to protect the game from its enemies in its own household, was Mr. Freedman's move to syndicate Base Ball."[34] Spalding went on to portray himself as a tireless opponent of the trust, whose heroic efforts produced the result that "The would-be syndicate had to do something to turn back the tide of public indignation sweeping in from all quarters. . . . Everywhere the scheme was denounced as outrageous; and so the trust was forced to emerge from the cover into which its members had crept when the storm broke."[35]

Spalding's version was a gross distortion of the actual events. In fact, Spalding was no enemy of trusts. His sporting goods firm had engaged in anticompetitive activities, and he had already created a bicycle trust and served as its president in 1898.[36] It was also Spalding who had apparently first floated the idea of a baseball trust to National League owners. All that Freedman and his allies had done was come up with a detailed plan for the trust.[37] What Spalding did do, however, was to sense a change in the attitude toward trusts earlier than did his rivals and act accordingly. The 1890s had ended with the American public feeling antipathy toward the trusts but also feeling helpless to do anything about them. But the situation changed dramatically as the new century began to unfold. Journalists turned out hundreds of books and articles a year, helping to rouse the public to a state of alarm. Progressive crusaders like William Jennings Bryan fanned the flames, and the inauguration of Teddy Roosevelt completed a rapid transformation.[38]

The new public mood forced both sides in the struggle for baseball to backpedal furiously. All plans for a trust were abandoned and each side tried to portray the other as the advocate of the idea. It was Spalding, however, who did so first and waged what James Hardy Jr. termed the more effective "propaganda campaign."[39] As a result, Spalding "managed to stick Freedman and [John T.] Brush with the authorship of this outrageous scheme, and he successfully evaded responsibility for his own trust plans."[40] In his 1911 book, Spalding recounted a telling anecdote from his playing days in the 1870s. When Spalding was pitching, teammate and second baseman Ross Barnes would sometimes make the motion of tagging a runner at second base when in fact the tag had been narrowly missed. Barnes would acknowledge afterward that he had not applied the tag, but neither Spalding in the pitcher's box nor the umpire behind the plate could tell, so the runner was declared out. Spalding commented: "In this case Barnes fooled the umpire. He had fooled me. But down the line there were spectators who had not been fooled. They could see the runner was safe, and they howled. But was that a square deal? Was it fair play? The umpire *believed* he was right. I *believed* him to be right. Those who were in a position to see from an angle impossible to him and to me *knew* that he was wrong." Spalding continued, in one of his grand rhetorical flourishes, to link "the future success of the great American national game" with his assertion that "as Americans we are committed by nature to stand for 'fair play' . . . as men we believe in a 'square deal' for everybody."[41] Spalding's ostensible point was the fairly simple one that umpires ought to be treated with greater respect. But he had also put his finger on the theme that laid the foundation for improvements in umpiring and groundskeeping—and the concurrent adjustments to ownership—in the first decade of the twentieth century.

These three areas of change, in field conditions, umpiring, and ownership, were each rooted not just in the principle of fair play but more specifically in the idea nicely conveyed by Spalding's image—that, in order for justice to be done, *it must be seen to be done*. In baseball's early days, the game did not receive intense scrutiny; merely giving both sides an opportunity to win had been sufficient. By the early twentieth century, baseball had reached a point where giving both sides a chance to win was no longer enough: the game's increased visibility meant that it had to go further and ensure that there was no vantage point from which obvious inequity could be perceived.

This change is why men like the Murphys played such an important role in the sport. By leveling playing fields, adding umpires, and eliminating dual ownership, baseball again enabled fans to see the game as fair. In so doing, it aligned itself with an egalitarian ideology that would come to dominate the twentieth century. The trusts were so unpopular because they suppressed competition. The challenge of the American League forced the National League to recognize that fans now expected from baseball a level playing field that would guarantee fair competition. Though a more accurate word for this idea would be a meritocracy, Spalding characteristically found a more emotionally resonant term. He called it democracy: "The genius of our institutions is democratic; Base ball is a democratic game. . . . We are a cosmopolitan people, knowing no arbitrary class distinctions, acknowledging none. The son of a President of the United States would as soon play ball with Patsy Flannigan as with Lawrence Lionel Livingstone, provided only that Patsy could put up the right article."[42]

It is no coincidence that Spalding chose an aristocratic English name and an unmistakably Irish name to illustrate his point.

4. Who'll Stop the Rain?

While Tom Murphy rapidly ascended to a position of prominence in baseball, his older brother John took a more circuitous route to the top. In 1885, John Murphy and several other Indianapolis ballplayers, including John's brother Pat and pitcher Toad Ramsey, went south to join the Birmingham (Alabama) club of the newly formed Southern Association.[1] Ramsey and Pat Murphy flashed the skills that would eventually get them to the major leagues, but John Murphy failed to make the team. He and two other Indianapolis ballplayers, Phil Corridan and Harry Smith, stayed on in Birmingham and played for an independent team known as the Theatre Comique Base Ball Club.[2] In addition to manning left field for the Theatre Comique club, John Murphy began a new career when the Birmingham Southern Association club hired him as a groundskeeper.

John Murphy pursued his new trade with Louisville of the American Association in 1886 and an independent club in Evansville, Indiana, in 1887. In 1888, Murphy was offered an opportunity he couldn't refuse. Indianapolis department store owner John T. Brush had acquired a National League franchise and wanted John Murphy to attend to the grounds of his hometown team. Murphy's whereabouts in 1889 are less clear, but he probably remained in Indianapolis and may have recommended that the club sign future Hall of Fame pitcher Amos Rusie. In 1890 John Murphy was reunited with his brother Pat as groundskeeper for St. Paul of the Western Association. He spent a total of three seasons in that league but each with a different club, following Pat to Minneapolis in 1891 and then on to Milwaukee the following season.[3]

Details about these years are sketchy, and some might assume from John Murphy's frequent moves that he had developed a reputation as a problem employee. Pittsburgh sportswriter A. R. Cratty would later observe of Murphy that "some of his side issues are not agreeable to the average employer."[4] This might be taken to imply a specific problem, such as alcoholism, yet there is little in his career to support that possibility. He was sometimes referred to as "Red" during these years, and no doubt appeared to many to be a stereotypical fiery Irishman. Several incidents confirm that Murphy had a hot temper, a trait that may have led observers to see him as the embodiment of the Irishman described in their schoolbooks—"passionate, ignorant, vain, and superstitious." There is, however, no hint of undependability or erratic behavior and thus no reason to believe that he had a drinking problem.

In addition, no fewer than three of Murphy's clubs—Birmingham, Minneapolis, and Milwaukee—folded before the end of the season in which Murphy had joined them. Though it was not uncommon for minor league clubs to fold, John Murphy was certainly unlucky to have three of his first four minor league clubs disband![5] It is safe to assume that his paychecks stopped as soon as the clubs folded—if not before—and that these experiences were a factor in his tendency to move on.

Murphy's stint in Minneapolis must have been especially aggravating. In August, with the club in first place, Minneapolis owner Henry Louis "Baron" Hach disbanded the team for no clear reason. The players were "naturally sore" about being abruptly thrust out of work, according to the local paper, "but all's well that ends well, and they have all got good berths for the remainder of the season."[6] But all was definitely not well for a groundskeeper under such circumstances, since no job vacancies were to be found at that time of year. Although no record exists to tell us John Murphy's activities for the rest of the year or how he took the news, we get a pretty good sense from two notes that appeared in the *Sporting Life* on the eve of the 1892 season. The Minneapolis correspondent lamented that the departure of "Superintendent Murphy" had cost the local team "the best ground keeper she ever had." The result was that the Minneapolis "grounds are not in as good shape as they were last spring." Meanwhile, the Milwaukee correspondent crowed in the very same issue that "Jack Murphy is doing splendid work at Athletic Park. He has had the outfield plowed and rolled, put in new runways and leveled the infield. Vice President Bartlett has given Murphy carte blanche regarding the grounds, and Murphy is taking advantage." The writer then added that the groundskeeper's motivation was intensified by an emotion that would recur later in his career: "Murphy's ambition is to make Baron Hach sick with envy when he comes down with the Flour City boys."[7]

It seems more likely then that John Murphy was simply a man who took great pride in his work and demanded more respect than groundskeepers of his era typically received. An unhappy consequence of the precarious financial footing of minor league clubs was that paychecks were always small and often intermittent. For example, as late as 1906, it was reported that highly regarded minor league groundskeeper Thomas Cooper was finally putting his foot down and demanding a regular monthly salary instead of the longstanding plan, which was "to pay him wages when the team was in town and let him root hog when it was away."[8] John Murphy was not the sort of man to cheerfully accept that kind of arrangement. Thus, the most likely explanation for his frequent moves is a quest for a place where he could receive the respect he felt he was due. The fact that he was never out of work suggests that the valuation he placed on his work was entirely justified.

Whatever their reason, John Murphy's travels continued. One later recap of his career indicated that he started the 1893 season as groundskeeper for Cap Anson's Chicago club.[9] Anson's notorious bigotry toward African Americans extended just as much to the Irish, and he was not reluctant about expressing his views.[10] It is plausible to imagine Murphy taking offense and resigning, but this is just speculation;

there is no confirmation that the stint in Chicago took place at all. At any rate, Murphy was working for the Erie club by May 1893 and drawing rave reviews for his labors on that low-lying baseball diamond. In June, the local *Sporting Life* correspondent reported: "Groundkeeper Murphy has done heroic work upon what a few weeks ago looked like an impossibility. He had a veritable sand bank to transform into a ball park. . . . The recent floods about undone everything for him, but with that determination and good judgment that has characterized his former good work he set right to work and to-day no trace of the water's work can be seen." Both home and visiting players pronounced them the best grounds anywhere.[11]

Erie captured the Eastern League pennant, and John Murphy found that recognition is doled out more generously after a championship. He expressed gratitude for his reception in Erie, which he called the best treatment he'd received in his fourteen years.[12] The statement is a curious one, since this was at most his ninth year as a baseball groundskeeper. Perhaps he was including earlier experience as a landscape gardener or maybe it was just that nine years as a groundskeeper felt like fourteen years! Murphy accepted a job in an Erie iron factory that winter, but let it be known that he was not committed to remaining in Erie in 1894. There were reports that he wanted to return to the Western Association and that he might go back to Milwaukee.[13] These statements sound suspiciously like negotiating ploys, and if so, Murphy must have eventually got what he wanted. The opening of the next season brought the welcome news from Erie that "Jack Murphy has been hard at work on the finest ball park in the League."[14]

A minor league town could not expect to hold on to such a skilled groundskeeper indefinitely. At the end of the 1894 season, Murphy received offers from two National League clubs. He turned down Philadelphia's offer when the two sides could not agree on a salary and instead signed a contract with Washington owners George and J. Earl Wagner that called for him to report for work on March 1. The advantages of being back in the major leagues were evident: a "force of laborers" helped him to prepare National Park for the season.[15]

Murphy's deft touch was immediately apparent: "Although he has only been at work seven days a wonderful change has come over the surface of the entire plot of ground," the *Washington Post* reported. "It will be a smoother and firmer surface this season than it has ever been before, and these points will not fail of appreciation by both the home and visiting players."[16] The groundskeeper expressed confidence that National Park would soon be the finest ballpark in the country.

The situation in the city Murphy had rejected was not as bright. The Philadelphia club had dismissed groundskeeper George Heubel after the 1894 season because they held him responsible for a disastrous fire. But the closer they came to the start of the 1895 season, the more evident it became that the club had erred in not agreeing to Murphy's demands. A last-minute flurry of expenditures only made things worse, as many opening-day spectators found their clothes ruined by the fresh paint on the seats. Philadelphia owner John I. Rogers soon approached the new Washington groundskeeper with a better offer. In April, this summary of the results appeared in the *Sporting Life*: "The facts in the case are that Murphy, who signed his services to the Messrs. Wagner for the season lasting from March 1 to October 1, has been acting peculiarly for more than a week. He tried to get a release from his contract several times, which of course was denied him. He told several of the friends he has made about town that he had been offered a position at the Philadelphia Park, and would sacrifice a good deal to get away so he could accept Mr. Rogers' offer."[17]

Exactly what transpired next is unclear, but John Murphy appears to have gotten his wish soon afterward. By July, a man named Miller was serving as Washington groundskeeper, and in September, the Philadelphia players were not able to use their dressing room because "Groundkeeper Murphy" was quarantined there with smallpox.[18] This was followed shortly after the season by word that "Groundkeeper Murphy will start laying out the Phillies diamond next week and will quit the profession if it's not the best field in the country."[19] He was not destined for a long stay in Philadelphia. His whereabouts in 1896 are unknown. He may still have been in Philadelphia, or it's possible he spent the season in either Columbus or Butte, both of which were listed in later summaries of his career. In any event, Murphy spent the 1897 season working for Buffalo of the Eastern League. At the end of that season, the Pittsburgh groundskeeper, "Old Tom," had to be hospitalized. His was an unforgiving vocation, however, and on December 13, 1897, John Murphy was hired to replace Old Tom.[20]

In making their choice, the Pittsburgh management undoubtedly took into account John Murphy's determined nature and the variety of skills he possessed. It seems safe to assume, however, that one factor was foremost in their minds—his work at Erie's flood-plagued ball park in 1893 and 1894. For his new place of employment, Exposition Park, stood on the banks of the Allegheny and Monongahela rivers. Of all the obstacles faced by nineteenth-century groundskeepers, none was more disheartening than rain. A groundskeeper always worked with one eye to the heavens, knowing that rain could erase every trace of that day's efforts and that flooding could obliterate the work of many weeks and months.

Moreover, the stakes were extremely high. Fields naturally varied greatly in their ability to handle rain, but few had good drainage. An 1868 account, for instance, noted that a game should have been scheduled for "the Capitoline grounds, which are fit to be played on a few hours after rain; but instead the meeting was appointed for the Union grounds at Tremont and rain the night previous had nearly [sic] the field a swamp."[21] Similarly, Henry Chadwick reported with approval in 1870 that the new field of the Olympic Club of Washington DC was "level and dry and can be played upon within two hours after a heavy rain."[22] Obviously, if the standard for good drainage was a field that was playable a few hours after rain, then on a poorly drained field a single day's rain could prevent play for days. This meant that groundskeepers were not the only ones who were always keeping an eye on the clouds. As a sportswriter explained in 1885, "clubs are almost bankrupt before they go into the field, and if bad weather overtakes them they are at once plunged into debt."[23]

Club owners were thus acutely aware of the weather and would do everything possible to avoid losing games to rain, especially if a large crowd was expected. A deliciously symbolic illustration of this took place in an April 16, 1891, exhibition game in which the Cedar Rapids club of the Two-I League was scheduled to host Chicago's famed National League club. Heavy rains had rendered the field a mess, but the appearance of a major league club was such a financial windfall for a minor league team that the game went ahead. During it, Cedar Rapids outfielder Henry Fabian reached base, and a hit sent him around third base with visions of the glorious feat of scoring a run against a major league club. Unfortunately, Fabian strayed from the safety of the base path and became stuck in the thick mud. While he was struggling to get himself free, he was tagged out, and Chicago went on to win 2–0.[24]

Naturally, Fabian's Cedar Rapids teammates never let him forget about the incident. One of those teammates was a teenaged infielder named John J. McGraw who would later hire Fabian to succeed John Murphy as head groundskeeper of the Polo Grounds. When McGraw's widow wrote her memoirs in 1953, she recounted this event faithfully (in stark contrast to her highly inaccurate recollections of John Murphy, which are described in this book's afterword).[25] So it seems safe to assume that whenever a patch of mud appeared on the field, Fabian was reminded of that memorable day in Cedar Rapids.

The ever-present threat of flooding made club owners extremely reluctant to invest money in ballparks; in Emerson's formulation, they remained tents rather than pyramids. So the burden fell on groundskeepers to create a ballpark that satisfied the demands of ballplayers, club owners, and spectators. At the same time, they were given only the most minimal resources with which to work. With the financial stakes so high, by the late nineteenth century baseball groundskeepers were increasingly focusing their attentions on preventing flooding. In this regard, they were again paralleling a major trend in Americans' larger struggle with their natural surroundings.

Having tamed a considerable amount of the country's vast wilderness, Americans were beginning to turn their attentions to dams and levees in order to exert similar control over the country's mighty rivers. The timing of these new pursuits was a function of the history of the country's settlement. Communities were usually established close to waterways, since this was the primary mode for transporting goods. The first settlers naturally selected the most promising farmland, which was usually high ground, and the communities grew outward. Only when the villages began to overflow did the low-lying land begin to be populated, making it essential to tame the rivers. Nor did the issue go away after a town had been settled. The need to manipulate water made it necessary to build diversion ditches and irrigation canals, and it was often for these tasks that Irish immigrants were brought in.

Baseball clubs watched these developments with a special interest. With the prime urban land already spoken for, ballparks were increasingly being built in low-lying areas on the outskirts of town. The good news was that these areas were being opened up to development by the streetcars. But in choosing such locations, ball clubs were rolling the dice. For example, the home park of the National Association's Westerns of Keokuk, Iowa, was a pasture that, in William J. Ryczek's words, "was bounded—rather, encroached upon—by Pleasant Lake."[26] Similarly, newspaper descriptions of Hamilton Field, home of the Kekiongas of Fort Wayne in the early 1870s, mentioned the "ever-present Menaces of the St. Mary's River."[27] Such menaces were more the rule than the exception. It was consequently the rare ballpark that wasn't susceptible to flooding.

A typical example occurred in Cincinnati when the Red Stockings joined the American Association in 1882 and secured grounds on Bank Street. Flooding disrupted both of the club's first two seasons, and then the ballpark was wrested from them by the rival Union Association. After considerable effort, the Red Stockings found a new home three blocks to the south, on a site that remained the home of Cincinnati baseball until 1970.[28] This location raised concerns, since it had once been "an old brickyard on Western Avenue, with ponds of various sizes, where the boys would amuse themselves wading and throwing mud at each other."[29] A local sportswriter optimistically noted that the new site was higher than the surrounding ground and therefore safer from flooding. He acknowledged that the area had been flooded the previous spring, "when nothing escaped the flood," but reported that prior to then it had not been under water since 1852.[30] Instead, both ballparks were again flooded in February by the second-worst flood in the city's history.[31]

The proximity of the Red Stockings' new park to the Ohio River ensured that the threat of flooding always lurked. The ground behind second base was raised so much that shortstops and second basemen regularly fell down when they ran over the "turtle back" in pursuit of shallow fly balls.[32] A 1901 game was able to proceed only because Reds groundskeeper John Schwab constructed a dike that was reportedly "made up out of a composition of rye bread, cement, brass filings, cheese, sawdust, sour beer, and wooden planks." Despite his efforts, a lake formed in the outfield, and balls hit into the flooded area were considered doubles. Schwab waded into the dingy water in his rubber boots and retrieved the balls.[33] Though Schwab's dike was literal, it seems likely that his dike's list of ingredients was at least partially tongue-in-cheek. Tongue-in-cheek accounts were common in this period, and it is often difficult to distinguish what is real and what is fabricated. But the image of Schwab's dike does convey the reality that the tools nineteenth-century groundskeepers had for combating rain and flooding were primitive.

"Turtle backs" like the one behind second base in Cincinnati were common, since the need for drainage was deemed more important than the difficulties thereby posed for fielders.[34] According to the *Chicago Tribune*, at a diamond in Memphis efforts to "produce a water shed against heavy showers and possible floods" literally transformed the field into a pyramid and created a bizarre impediment: "second base is much lower than the plate but in order to throw there the catcher must elevate his sights so as to clear the hurler's ridge."[35]

In 1884, St. Louis groundskeeper August Solari had introduced what Henry Chadwick described as "an improvement which might be copied to advantage. It is the placing of tarpaulins over the four base positions to protect them from wet weather."[36] The idea was indeed widely copied, and soon extended to cover the pitcher's box and sometimes the baseline.[37] But this still left much of the field uncovered, and drying a wet field remained a daunting task. Some groundskeepers used fire engines to pump the field, and others burned oil or gasoline, either of which would have been an appropriate activity for the Murphys. A more common practice was to scatter sawdust in the wet areas.[38] Sawdust was an imperfect way to dry a field, but its use would have far-reaching consequences. An 1885 article, for example, observed that "When the Trenton team reached the Hartford ground yesterday, they found five men with sponges hard at work on the diamond, and [pitcher Mike] Tiernan was mounted on a pile of sawdust."[39] It is from such improvisations that the baseball mound developed.

It is more difficult to pinpoint which club was the first to recognize that such heaps of sawdust could be used not merely for drainage but to gain a home field advantage. There is, however, good reason to think that the Orioles and Tom Murphy played a major role. Hugh Fullerton recalled in 1906 that during the Orioles' heyday, "The pitcher's box was a foot higher than the plate."[40] Though there is no specific contemporary confirmation of this statement, some compelling circumstantial evidence supports it. When longtime Baltimore manager Ned Hanlon transferred himself and most of his stars to Brooklyn in 1899, he immediately "raised his pitcher's box nearly one foot, making it difficult for the visiting players. The home players are able to overcome the handicap by practice."[41] It thus seems logical to take Fullerton's word that Hanlon had used the same tactic in Baltimore. The mound did not gain acceptance without a fight. Giants manager Buck Ewing objected that "Hanlon has no more right to raise his pitcher's box a foot than New York has a right to dig a trench one foot deep from the home plate to the pitcher's box at the Polo Grounds."[42]

It thus seems likely that Tom Murphy played a major role in the development of the pitcher's mound. If so, it is apt that the man so associated with uneven fields had helped to introduce the one area of today's diamond that is not level. The following year, *Sporting Life*'s Cleveland correspondent reported that "one of the secrets of the success of the Cleveland Club at home came to light" in a game on August 25. The writer explained:

> Some time ago "The News" had a story regarding the effective pitching in the League this season, and gave as the reason the fact that in the different park the pitcher's box was raised from one to two feet, thus enabling the pitchers to throw down hill, and get not only more speed, but better control as well. This is the case in every city except Cleveland.
>
> Here the batters' box has been raised nearly twelve inches above the pitchers' slab, and the boxmen are forced to throw up-hill. The Cleveland pitchers, working at home half the time, have thoroughly mastered the difference in the two positions, and can, by reason of the fact that they work oftener at home than on any other one field, have much greater command of the ball and know exactly how to work the variations in their delivery. The question of relative positions of the plate and pitcher's box with the other parts of the diamond is one which just now is of much interest, and will be discussed at the annual meetings this fall.[43]

The issue was undoubtedly the subject of heated debate, but it was hard to legislate against any tactic that had the potential to make a field more playable. The result was that no action was taken against pitchers' mounds, and other clubs began to imitate Brooklyn.

With mounds now established, Hanlon became still more brazen in his approach. In 1901, he made use of a noteworthy tactic whenever Christy Mathewson was scheduled to pitch in Brooklyn. According to Mathewson, "Every time he thought I was going to pitch there, he would have the diamond doctored for me in the morning. The groundkeeper sank the pitcher's box down so that it was below the level of all the bases instead of slightly elevated as it should be." When Mathewson complained to Giants manager George S. Davis, he was told "never mind. When we are entertaining, the box at the Polo Grounds will be built up the days you are going to pitch against Brooklyn, and you can burn them over and at their heads if you like."[44]

Until this point, tampering with mounds had been done primarily to create a surface that would be comfortable for the home pitchers and uncomfortable for the visiting pitcher. Gradually, however, the idea that mounds gave pitchers an advantage gained currency, and special requests from pitchers caused groundskeepers to put all the more time into crafting them. A *Sporting Life* correspondent observed that during the 1902 season, "every ground in the Eastern League had a raised pitcher's box, and it increased the power of the slabmen."[45]

In 1903, some action was finally taken when the rule that mounds could not exceed fifteen inches in height was instituted. This, however, was a timid move since it only mandated a maximum height. Clubs could still raise or lower the mound to their heart's contents within that range, and it was not until 1950 that the major leagues first required that all mounds be of uniform height. This lengthy delay shows that rule makers understood the importance of giving groundskeepers the greatest flexibility in combating their greatest enemy—rain.

Although all groundskeepers lived in fear of flooding, this sober reality also ensured that one who was experienced in battling floods would be in constant demand. And so it was that John Murphy started the 1898 season with Pittsburgh.

5. A Diamond Situated
in a River Bottom

John Murphy's new home, Pittsburgh's Exposition Park, had an intriguing history. The Allegheny Exposition was an annual event that began in 1875 as a way of promoting western Pennsylvania's trades and industries. One of its features was an oval track for bicycle and horse races, which was converted to baseball by Pittsburgh's entry in the American Association's maiden season of 1882.[1] Most of the exposition buildings were destroyed by fire in 1883. The racetrack-ballpark was salvaged, but a year later the baseball club moved to a new home. In 1890, the upstart Players' League brought major league baseball back to the site of the exposition. Their stadium proved appealing enough that, when the Players' League folded, the National League Pirates took up occupancy in 1891.

Although the location of Exposition Park was a convenient one for most purposes, it had one drawback that sometimes overwhelmed all of the benefits. It was situated near the confluence of the Allegheny and Monongahela rivers, with the outfield fence only 250 feet from the former.[2] The results were predictable: "It takes a good man to keep old Expo Park in shape for the many freshets that deluge the field and leave a layer of mud are harassing," local scribe A. R. Cratty commented. "A man will just about get the field in shape some days when up comes the old Allegheny, and it's all off."[3] Worse, the water was liable to freeze, causing further inconvenience and delay.

Exposition Park's watershed status gave John Murphy plenty of opportunities to make use of his previous experience with flooding. He also borrowed some tricks from his younger brother, as Chicago catcher Tim Donahue noted:

> Pittsburg has a diamond situated in a river bottom and by the 1st of July that diamond is like an asphalt street. Second base is six feet lower than the home plate and first and third each three feet lower. The lines to first and third are banked up like the cushions on a billiard table. Some people think that will not give Pittsburg the advantage, but when one comes to study the Pittsburg team he will see what I mean. . . . When that diamond bakes hard those fellows will beat dozens of infield hits, for every man can bunt, and most of them can chop the ball, and they will win almost every close game.[4]

The Pirates didn't really need such help, having already started to assemble the nucleus of the team that succeeded the Orioles as the National League's dominant club. Their ascendance had been prompted by one of the many dubious moves of the syndicate era. With the National League intent on ridding itself of his franchise (for reasons that will be discussed in the next chapter), Louisville owner Barney Dreyfuss had initiated a bold transaction. The thirty-four-year-old German immigrant bought nearly half of the Pirates and then transferred fourteen of his players to Pittsburgh, including stars Honus Wagner, Fred Clarke, Tommy Leach, and Deacon Phillippe. The transfusion of talent enabled Pittsburgh to finish second in 1900, and Dreyfuss then bought a controlling share. Recognizing the potential for a dynasty, Dreyfuss was generous with his players, and he reaped the rewards. His club kept all of its key players while its rivals were being hit hard by American League raids. The result was that the Pirates captured three straight pennants from 1901 to 1903.

Dreyfuss also initially recognized the value of his groundskeeper and when John Murphy came aboard extended his generosity to him as well. A later account noted: "The Pirate management considered him so valuable that they built him a home way out in center field, and when it was swept away once by a Spring flood, the management not only rebuilt Murphy's house but refurbished it as well."[5] Undoubtedly, such recognition was one major reason why Pittsburgh became the first city in which John Murphy stayed for more than two seasons.

Though John Murphy must have experienced great satisfaction during his stay in Pittsburgh, it was not exactly a case of basking in the glow. Many chores fell to the groundskeeper, but basking was never one of them! John Murphy was asked before the 1901 season, for example, to raise the entire infield so it would drain more easily after the periodic floods. His labors did accomplish this end, but the infield became unduly hard: "The deposits of last spring and then the raising of the infield have made the field as hard as a brickwalk at times, and the ball shoots off sharply," the *Sporting Life*'s correspondent reported. "Each day the diamond is given a liberal sprinkling, but this does not seem to obviate the liveliness."[6] Then in December 1901, the ballpark was hit with a deluge that caused even Murphy to remark, "I have seen many speedy floods, but this last one was a real corker." He had warily looked on all evening from his home at the ballpark as the nearby water levels rose to dangerous heights. At 10:00 p.m., he telephoned sportswriter John H. Gruber to find out if the Signal Service—the branch of the army that issued severe weather warnings—was anticipating a flood. Only an hour later, his eyes gave him all the information he needed. He finally escaped in the nick of time: "About 11 o'clock I made up my mind to get out, and I did. Just about 2 a.m. in came the water in my house. The highest was about the top of the grand stand rail."[7]

Murphy set about repairing the damage and accomplished as much as he could, but work on the grounds had to be deferred until spring.[8] Unfortunately, the waters returned before the spring came: "Thirty-one feet of water again" was the ominous news. "Groundkeeper Murphy was on to this flood and got out of Expo Park in plenty of time. He had his eye on the river early in the evening. The water raised to the top row in the grand stand."[9] Within a month of this latest flood,

Murphy had left the Pirates' employ under mysterious circumstances. He was initially said to have resigned, but reports soon surfaced that his departure was the result of friction with management.[10] Pittsburgh sportswriter A. R. Cratty, however, later reported that the change was precipitated by a feud between Murphy and star pitcher Deacon Phillippe. According to Cratty, "Phil [Deacon Phillippe] caught onto the fact that a side gate was being used by many unauthorized persons to gain entrance, and so reported. This led to a fly around, which resulted in a change of ground keeper."[11]

This account is difficult to reconcile with the fact that Murphy's departure occurred immediately before the start of the season. The only possibility is that Phillippe's accusations reached Barney Dreyfuss belatedly and that when he confronted Murphy with them, Murphy responded by either quitting or forcing Dreyfuss to fire him. It is known that Murphy harbored great resentment for Dreyfuss, as he once stopped at Exposition Park on his way through town only after making sure that Dreyfuss was not around.[12]

Whatever the reason, John Murphy left his first long-term engagement in March 1902, and it would be several years before he again found an enduring home.

6. Tom Murphy's Crime

The upturn in John Murphy's fortunes when he was hired by Pittsburgh was directly paralleled by a decline in Tom's. The December 11, 1897, issue of *Sporting Life* reported both John Murphy's engagement with the Pirates and some extensive improvements that Tom Murphy was making at Baltimore's Union Park. These included elevating the ground between first and second base a foot and a half to make it even with third base and raising right field five feet so that right fielder Willie Keeler would no longer be lower than the plate.[1] No reason was given for eliminating characteristics that had previously been viewed as advantages. It is possible that complaints from rival owners played a role. A more likely scenario is that the changes were deemed necessary for drainage—as noted in chapter 5, John Murphy would later make similar changes at the perpetually waterlogged Exposition Park. Union Park had similar problems because of an old stream known as Brady's Run that ran directly behind the right field fence. As a result, water regularly oozed under the fence and "created a perpetual swamp in right field."[2]

Yet even if these changes were necessary, the voluntary elimination of an apparent advantage symbolized that the Orioles were beginning to lose the competitive edge that had been their hallmark. In 1898, the club finished second, and it was clear that the team's nucleus could not be kept together much longer. It was not so much that the club was getting old as that they had played the game so hard that their bodies were wearing out. John McGraw and Hughey Jennings, who had conducted off-season drills in which they practiced allowing themselves to be hit by pitches, were the most obvious examples. McGraw was only twenty-five at the close of the 1898 season, but he had already put his slight five-feet-seven-inch frame through as much torment as it could endure. Plagued by a series of injuries, he would remain a regular for only another two and a half seasons.

Jennings was in even worse shape. He had been hit by pitches over two hundred times in the five previous seasons, a mark never since approached by anyone in baseball history. His skull was fractured in 1897 by an Amos Rusie pitch, although typically Jennings played another inning before coming out of the game.[3] With the adoption of batting helmets and other protective equipment still in the future, he undoubtedly suffered an endless string of other bruises. Yet it was a very different type of injury that proved his undoing. After one of the greatest five-year runs that a shortstop has ever experienced, Jennings came up with a lame arm. Characteristically, his injury was simply the result of working too hard. Tom Murphy later recalled: "Hanlon would order me to stop morning practice at 11 o'clock. Everyone would be willing to quit but Jennings. I could not get him off the field with a team of mules. I have taken away all the bats, turned the hose on the diamond, confiscated the balls, but could not succeed in making him desist."[4] Today's doctors would in all likelihood diagnose Jennings's condition as a torn rotator cuff and repair it surgically. But there were no such options in the 1890s, and Jennings's days as a regular shortstop were over, though he would move to first base and play for a few more years.

As a result, the 1898 season ended with challenges looming for the Orioles. The club had surmounted imposing obstacles before, but this time would be different and for a disturbing reason. Team owners Harry von der Horst and Ned Hanlon made the fateful decision to all but abandon the pretext of competitiveness. They had become dissatisfied with the Baltimore public's support of their great team and had even transferred some games to other locales in 1898. Before the

1899 season, they became part of the game's movement toward syndicate baseball by acquiring an interest in the Brooklyn team and trying to turn their new club into a champion at the expense of the old one. Hanlon moved to Brooklyn along with such stars as Jennings, Keeler, and Joe Kelley. McGraw and Wilbert Robinson declined to move because they owned a lucrative tavern and eatery in Baltimore, so it was agreed to leave them behind to supervise the remnants of the dynasty.

Predictably, the infusion of talent allowed Brooklyn to capture the 1899 pennant. What was more surprising was that the stripped-down Baltimore roster remained highly competitive. McGraw had cannily kept management from recognizing the potential of a young pitcher named Joe McGinnity, who would lead the league with twenty-eight victories. McGraw piloted the Orioles to an 86-61 mark in 1899, but it wasn't enough to save the franchise. Following the 1899 season, the National League acknowledged that the "big league" had been a mistake and scaled back to eight clubs. Baltimore was one of the casualties.

Tom Murphy was not around for the final season. The exact date and reasons for his departure are unknown, but it seems reasonable to assume that a club that was ridding itself of first-rate playing talent wasn't willing to pay competitive wages to a groundskeeper. There were plenty of clubs that were, however, and Murphy spent the 1899 season in St. Louis. Tom Murphy had found a home at Baltimore's Union Park—both literally and figuratively, for like his brother he slept in a cottage on the grounds.[5] After leaving Baltimore, he would never again find a permanent home. Following one season in St. Louis, he signed to be groundskeeper for Ned Hanlon's Brooklyn team, only to change his mind a week after his arrival and return to St. Louis.[6] In 1901, he was hired to care for the grounds of the Philadelphia entry in the National League's latest rival, the American League.

As with so many other elements of baseball history, land played a vital role in the emergence of this new league, one that is easily overlooked. By the late 1890s, the increasingly unpopular uses that National League owners were making of their monopoly led to discussions about forming a rival major league. But these efforts remained only talk until the end of the century, and the reasons were once again rooted in baseball's need for a sizable amount of land. The National League's occupancy of twelve of the nation's largest cities left any potential rival with two unpalatable alternatives. The first was to place franchises in smaller cities, which would make it difficult to convince the press and the public that it was a serious rival to the National League. It would also limit revenues, making it very difficult to attract star players. The second option was to compete head to head in National League cities, but this course was also fraught with peril. One of the main problems was that there were few suitable locations for a baseball stadium in most cities, and the existing team already had the best site. Additionally, a new team would be competing against a team and players that already held the city's allegiance. Moreover, lingering memories of the failure of the Players' League in 1890 would make it very difficult to attract the funding necessary for a direct challenge.

The situation changed during the 1899 season, however, when it became common knowledge that the National League planned to drop four franchises —Louisville, Cleveland, Washington, and Baltimore— at season's end. It was suddenly viable to envision an eight-city rival major league that would have four to six significant markets to itself, while competing directly with the National League in only a few select cities where conditions were favorable. No sooner had the 1899 campaign ended than a concerted effort was begun to revive the American Association for the 1900 season. The enterprise had a lot of advantages going for it. There was no shortage of disgruntled National Leaguers, and the rival league quickly lined up big names such as Cap Anson and John McGraw as prime movers. It also gained the important support of the founders and longtime editors of both major sporting papers, *Sporting Life*'s Francis C. Richter and *Sporting News*'s Alfred H. Spink.[7]

The plans for the new league called for a balanced mix of cities. There would be three new cities (Providence, Milwaukee, and Detroit) and two National League castoffs (Baltimore and Louisville), and three cities were to be the stage for the all-important head-to-head competition. The scarcity of land and the fact that there were already clubs in New York and Brooklyn made New York City impractical. This left only three viable options: Boston, Chicago, and Philadelphia. In spite of the new rival's advantages, major obstacles had to be overcome. The National League was well aware of the impending threat and did its best to thwart the would-be rivals. Though the senior league was committed to dropping its four weakest franchises, it delayed making a formal announcement to make things as difficult as possible for the American Association.

A particularly bizarre scene took place in Baltimore, where Hanlon and von der Horst had let the lease on Union Park expire. McGraw obtained a lease on the ballpark, but the old owners were not giving up so easily. They stationed armed guards at the gates and even occupied the clubhouse and Tom Murphy's old cottage, forcing McGraw to get a court order to evict them.[8] As it turned out, the new league would fail as a direct result of another problem involving land. In February, the principal backer of the Philadelphia franchise informed McGraw that he had not yet found a suitable ballpark. When McGraw passed the information along, Anson announced the demise of the new American Association before it had played a single game. Only then did the National League officially acknowledge its intention to cut back to eight clubs in 1900.[9]

All of these moves and countermoves had been carefully observed by Western League president Ban Johnson, an ambitious thirty-six-year-old former sportswriter. The Western League was a strong minor league with eight franchises in the expanding region now known as the Midwest. The westward course of the U.S. population provided reason to hope that the Western League might eventually evolve into a major league. But Johnson recognized that the National League's desertion of four viable markets gave him the chance to accelerate the process. He also realized that there was nothing wrong with the new American Association's plan. The upstart league's failure had just been a matter of lacking enough time to find the right backers and the right locations for ballparks.

Accordingly, Johnson moved with an astute combination of speed and deliberateness. He moved franchises to Chicago and Cleveland and changed the league's name to the American League in 1900. But he also cannily bought himself a full year to build and plan by continuing to operate the circuit as a minor league. The Chicago franchise gained the National League's approval by agreeing to locate south of 35th Street and to refrain from using the word *Chicago* in its name.[10] At the end of the 1900 season, Johnson approached the National League about being recognized as a major league. When he was rebuffed, he was prepared for the war he was about to wage. His teams commenced raids on National League players, honoring existing contracts for the 1901 season but not the controversial reserve clause.

The American League's geographic plan was closely modeled on that of the ill-fated new American Association. Two franchises—Detroit and Milwaukee—were longtime Western League stalwarts, and they would be joined by three National League castoffs, Cleveland, Washington, and Baltimore. This meant five dependable markets, but Johnson knew that the new league's fortunes would depend on successfully targeting National League cities that could support two ball clubs. The scarcity of land still made New York impractical, so he selected the same three cities as the American Association for head-to-head competition: Boston, Chicago, and Philadelphia.

With so much riding on the results, it was critical that the new league have talented leadership in these three cities. Ideally, men who had starred for their cross-town rivals would manage these clubs. Jimmy Collins, an established star for the Boston National League entry, was persuaded to take over the Boston Americans. Charles Comiskey had been manager and owner of the Chicago American League entry in 1900, but for 1901 he recruited the cross-town rival's veteran pitcher Clark Griffith to assume the reins. Comiskey then moved to the front office, thereby ensuring that both Boston and Chicago would be well-run clubs with a marquee gate attraction as manager. That left Philadelphia, which had no such obvious choice. Fortunately, an inspired selection was made when the job was given to a tall, thin, soft-spoken Irishman who had been managing Milwaukee in the Western League.

Cornelius McGillicuddy, better known as Connie Mack, would remain manager of the Athletics for half a century.

Mack undoubtedly thought that he had gotten a gem when he hired Tom Murphy as the club's groundskeeper, but the choice proved ill fated. On June 6, an assailant struck Mack's brother Dennis McGillicuddy over the head with a baseball bat in the club's dressing room and left him for dead. McGillicuddy suffered a fractured skull and hovered on the verge of death for several weeks.[11] He eventually survived, but had to have a silver plate inserted in his skull and never entirely recovered.[12] Suspicion immediately fell upon Tom Murphy. On the evening after the attack, he was arrested as he attempted to board a train for Cleveland. He was charged with "atrocious assault" and jailed. The circumstances of the attack remain murky, but it appears that McGillicuddy, in his capacity as the club's night watchman, had accused Murphy of theft. An argument ensued that ended in the assault.

Tom Murphy spent two months in jail before being released on $600 bail.[13] He promptly skipped bail and did not appear for trial. There was a sighting of him in Cincinnati, but he vanished again and spent the next year on the run from the law.[14] An American at the turn of the century who wanted to leave his past behind was usually able to do so. The FBI was not created until 1908, fingerprinting was in its infancy, and local police departments were inclined to feel they were fortunate if a criminal fled town. The likelihood that Murphy would ever be recaptured was remote at best, which makes what happened next all the more extraordinary.

The following summer, Connie Mack's Athletics were in St. Louis for a July 31 game. While walking around the town before the game, Mack passed Tom Murphy on the street. Recognizing his brother's assailant, Mack caught the attention of two policemen and they arrested the fugitive.[15] Murphy was returned to Philadelphia for trial, where he was represented by attorney Daniel Shern.[16] Not much of a defense could be made, however, and the groundskeeper was convicted of aggravated assault and battery. Tom Murphy was sentenced to two years and nine months in the penitentiary.[17]

7. Return to Exposition Park

John Murphy left his job as Pittsburgh groundskeeper in March 1902, and for the next two years he reverted to his earlier pattern of itinerancy as a groundskeeping vagabond. He first surfaced in Baltimore, with the American League franchise managed by John McGraw. John Murphy and John McGraw were both feisty Irishmen who seem to have achieved an immediate rapport.

John Murphy set about making his mark on Baltimore's new park with his characteristic vigor. In the process, he gave the field what was to become his trademark stamp, a look very different from the one associated with his brother. After tending to holes in the outfield and trouble spots in the infield, he added distinctive touches. "Around the grandstand the park resembles one of our public squares," the *Sporting Life*'s correspondent noted. "A large flower bed has been constructed at each end of the grandstand, and when the season opens it is expected that they will be filled with plants in full bloom."[1] The park's striking appearance was so well received that Murphy soon embellished it, as *Sporting Life* reported:

> Groundkeeper Murphy, of American League Park, has been hard at work improving and beautifying the grounds during the absence of the Baltimore club. One of the most striking improvements is the placing of a border of sod around the grounds in front of the grandstand, which

gives the entire grounds a neat finish. The flower beds to the right and left of the grandstand have been filled out with bright colored plants and flowers and vines have been planted along the front of the ladies' stand. A new design of sod has been made in front of the grandstand with the names McGraw and Robinson worked in sod. Under the designs are the words "Keep Off."[2]

Murphy also remained mindful of the unique environment in which he worked, positioning the flowers safely out of the way of foul popups.[3] In addition to making the "look 50% better than last year," Murphy again borrowed one of his brother's signature tricks to help McGraw's offense.[4] Visitors to Baltimore were soon complaining that "that ridge they have built up along third and first base lines helps them in their bunting, for a ball cannot roll foul in either line."[5] Unfortunately, the park's beautiful appearance was belied by the turmoil surrounding the club. John McGraw was feuding with American League president Ban Johnson and soon had had enough. After some extraordinarily convoluted machinations, McGraw bolted for New York to become manager of the Giants. No sooner was this accomplished than Giants owner Andrew Freedman gained a controlling interest in the Orioles and promptly released six key players. He immediately signed four of them for his New York club, with the other two joining John T. Brush's Cincinnati club. Ban Johnson had to step in and take charge of the Baltimore franchise just to keep the team and the league afloat.[6]

John Murphy was left behind, and the Orioles' situation must have brought back bitter memories of previous clubs that had not survived the season's end. It is said that Murphy got down on his hands and knees by the flowerbed where he had spelled out the name "McGraw" in white posies and in frustration tore up the posies one by one.[7] If the story is true, John Murphy must soon have had a change of heart. He stayed in Baltimore for a few weeks before receiving another blow with the news that Tom had been recaptured. Undoubtedly sensing that Baltimore was likely to be dropped from the American League at season's end, John Murphy followed McGraw to New York.

Upon his arrival in New York, Murphy told reporters that he would continue his practice of creating designs in the turf with one featuring the "Heavenly Twins"—McGraw and Giants owner Andrew Freedman.[8] His services during the remainder of 1902 were so valued by the Giants players that they presented him with a gold watch at season's end.[9] The following spring, Ned Hanlon brought baseball back to Baltimore with an Eastern League franchise and convinced John Murphy to return with him. In May, the groundskeeper's services again gained him special recognition. "The Baltimore officials and players have presented ground keeper Murphy with a massive gold watch chain and locket," *Sporting Life* explained. "The latter has in it a raised doe's head, under which there is a diamond."[10]

Yet within a month of the award John Murphy was moving on again, returning to another familiar destination. In the fifteen months since John Murphy's abrupt departure from Pittsburgh, Exposition Park had become "rather run down under the manipulation of other ground keepers."[11] Murphy's replacements had found the frequent flooding to be particularly bedeviling. Before an Independence Day doubleheader in 1902, rain had left knee-high water in the outfield. Because the holiday crowd represented so much revenue, the games were played anyway. Special ground rules were enacted for balls that landed in the waterlogged areas, and the outfielders had to cope as best they could. Brooklyn outfielder Cozy Dolan reportedly "took to the water like a duck. Out his way the flood was knee deep, but the Brooklyn center fielder simply reveled in aquatics."[12]

Pirates owner Barney Dreyfuss eventually realized that there was only one man who could be counted on to set things right and decided to bury the hatchet. As a result, sportswriter A. R. Cratty reported in June that "There is a familiar figure hustling about old Expo Park these days. John Murphy, the veteran ground keeper, is again in charge. . . . The management forgot the old feud and took on Murphy. The players are all pleased."[13] The results were predictable. John Murphy soon had the park in prime shape, and the players showed their gratitude by voting him a partial share of the World Series pot.[14]

Murphy's enhanced status was also reflected in the presence of a full-time assistant to whom Murphy occasionally turned over responsibility for sleeping at the ballpark. This proved fortuitous in October when Murphy was away on a hunting trip. Several nearby shops caught on fire and sparks began spreading to the wooden grandstands until the assistant doused them with his hose.[15]

But signs of tension were also emerging. Murphy was finding a variety of ways to earn a few extra dollars, suggesting that his salary remained a bone of contention. When football games were played at Exposition Park, he took advantage of his home in center field to earn extra money by boarding dogs, fixing broken chairs, and selling photos of Honus Wagner.[16] Another warning signal came when the employees of Exposition Park played a September exhibition game against a team made up of local writers. The writers were beaten 17–7, but they mischievously reversed the score in their accounts, while also charging their opponents with many spurious errors. As a former minor league player, John Murphy was irate to read that he had committed five errors. He was further enraged by an article claiming that writer John H. Gruber had beaten Murphy in a footrace, since Murphy had in fact won the race handily. Before the Pirates' next home game, Murphy erected a large sign reading, "Murphy won the foot race," and also chalked the same message on the field.[17]

After the season, John McGraw offered Murphy the opportunity to return to the Polo Grounds for the 1904 campaign. McGraw would undoubtedly have been happy to acquire Murphy's services under any circumstances but, given a feud that had simmered between the Pirates and Giants all year, he must have particularly relished the knowledge that he would be depriving Barney Dreyfuss of a key employee. The groundskeeper accepted McGraw's offer but remained at his old job until word of the arrangement leaked out. When the rumor reached the ears of Pirates secretary William Locke, he "investigated and learned that Murphy had accepted money from McGraw on account,"

Sporting Life reported. "Locke had the facts substantiated and then reasoned that Murphy should leave the Pittsburg Club December 30. He gave him his notice at once. This cut Murphy out of some salary."[18] But if Murphy endured a short-term loss, it was Dreyfuss who suffered more, and this loss undoubtedly contributed to the feud Dreyfuss continued to wage with McGraw for the next twenty years.[19]

With Murphy gone, Dreyfuss's plans to spruce up Exposition Park for the 1904 season were derailed. Planned changes to the field were abandoned because of the fear of flooding. An effort was made to paint the entire park, but the project was nowhere near completion on opening day. The half-painted look was such an eyesore that "management was compelled to place sheeting over the new painted surfaces," Cratty noted. "This work was only gotten up about a half hour before the gates were opened to a rousing crowd."[20] Exposition Park's vulnerability to the elements would continue to plague the groundskeepers who succeeded Murphy. In 1908, Barney Dreyfuss purchased for the park one of the first large-scale tarpaulins used in baseball, but this was only a partial solution. In the middle of the 1909 season he sought to resolve the issue by moving to higher ground at the newly built Forbes Field, one of a new wave of concrete-and-steel stadiums.

Even at Forbes Field, a "turtle back" continued to interfere with the play of pitchers and infielders. A 1914 article explained: "When the vast ball park was built a tremendous fill-in was needed just where the inner works are located. Wagon load after wagon load of fine packing soil was dumped into a ravine and the surface really made higher than needed for playing purposes, because the engineer expected a settling at this point. Some sagging occurred, but not so much as anticipated. Therefore the diamond is a trifle strong on elevation particularly behind the slabman's station. The peaked portion in ways hampered and harassed tossers."[21] Shortly before the Pirates' departure, Exposition Park gave them one last reminder of why they had sought new premises. Metaphorically inclined sportswriter I. E. Sanborn noted that the "foreboded elevation of Pittsburg's triumvirate of inland Neptunes" had caused the water levels to "[reach] the stage where the flood gates protecting B. Dreyfuss' plant were useless, and in a few hours everything except the humpbacked diamond was subaqueous—i.e. under water." Sanborn added, tongue in cheek, that "Capt. [Fred] Clarke and his pirate crew escaped from their irrigated camp by swimming the Monongahela at low tide and boarding a coal barge. At latest accounts all escaped drowning."[22]

Exposition Park was used between 1912 and 1915 by clubs in the rival United States and Federal Leagues, but then gradually fell into disuse. By 1970, however, the Allegheny had been channeled effectively enough for major league baseball to return to the site of John Murphy's labors. Three Rivers Stadium was built so close to the location of Exposition Park that members of the Society for American Baseball Research (SABR) were able to determine that the home plate of the old ballpark was located in Three Rivers parking lot number 4. They marked the historic site with spray paint.[23]

8. No Suitable Ground on the Island

In 1904, John Murphy returned to New York and John McGraw's Giants. Reunited with a kindred spirit, Murphy finally made the permanent home that his brother Tom had never been able to. Just like John Murphy, New York City's National League entries had undergone a long and arduous trek before finding a home at the Polo Grounds. To appreciate why Murphy's skills were so essential we need to first understand the "mucky details" of that history.

As we've seen, a distinguishing feature of the "New York game" was that it required less land than other bat-and-ball games. Yet, ironically, baseball would soon need more space than New York City could accommodate. Another irony was that recreation in New York City had begun to resemble that of England: land constraints had become the all-consuming factor. Other American cities were beginning to sprawl, but an island such as Manhattan had no such luxury and thus little room for outdoor leisure. The sole exception was Central Park, but its picturesque beauty had been made possible by generous government funding and the visionary design of Frederick Law Olmsted and Calvert Vaux. Baseball clubs could count on neither of these. As a result, in the 1860s and 1870s the city's baseball clubs almost always played their home games elsewhere. As noted in chapter 2, the Knickerbockers had already been crowded out of New York City and were using Hoboken's Elysian Fields. This remained a popular location for amateur clubs during the 1860s, but since it was not enclosed (fenced in or otherwise surrounded by boundaries) it was not practical for professional matches.[1]

The Unions of Morrisania, one of the top clubs of the late 1860s, selected a remote site fourteen miles north of the city in Tremont, Westchester County. The field was ringed by trees and railroad tracks, apt reminders of the conflicting requirements of an ideal site—distance from the city, yet close enough to draw spectators. The Tremont location was also well situated for access by boat and horsecar.[2] Unfortunately, even if the site was convenient for transportation, a fourteen-mile trek remained time consuming. Worse, the railway embankments impinged upon play because they left the playing area "shaped like a triangular segment of a circle," one observer noted, "fenced in on all sides with embankments, on which railroads are laid, and so small that while the catcher was obliged to play at the apex of the triangle the outfielders were compelled to stand close to the embankment at the lower part of the field and be ready to mount the bank in order to field the ball when batted over the railroad tracks, as very frequently happened."[3]

Because of these factors, ambitious clubs usually opted for Brooklyn (which was not considered part of New York City until 1898). In the 1850s, it was still possible to play on the "vacant fields then existing in South Brooklyn."[4] These began to vanish, but Brooklyn's Union Grounds (not to be confused with the park in Tremont) became popular because it offered the well-maintained enclosed field needed to attract paying spectators. A second enclosed ballpark, the Capitoline Grounds, was opened in Brooklyn in 1864. Enclosed ballparks paved the way for professional baseball in a very tangible way, since the walls made it possible to regularly collect admission, which had previously been done on only a few isolated occasions. The concept of professionalism was also linked to the game's "mucky details" in a less apparent manner. In the early 1860s, the public resisted the notion of paying to watch baseball games, an understandable reaction given that games had traditionally cost nothing.

Even efforts to charge admission by billing the contests as benefit games or by donating the proceeds to charities met limited success. As historian George Kirsch has suggested, one of the factors that helped to break down this resistance was arguing that an admission fee made possible "witnessing first-class nines contending on well cared for grounds."[5] This tactic cleverly deflected objections to paying for professional ball-playing by linking the concept to the more acceptable one of paying for good landscaping. This line of reasoning proved so persuasive that even some of the clubs that reverted to amateurism in the early 1870s charged admission fees to pay for upkeep of the grounds.[6]

Yet the hard-won public acceptance of the concept of admission fees was not enough to bring real estate prices in New York City within the means of the upstart game. New York City's entries in the National Association and National League played at Brooklyn's Union Grounds until the city's representative was expelled after the National League's inaugural season of 1876. When the nation's largest city gained readmission in 1883, its team finally had a field that was no longer away from home. In 1880, wealthy businessman John B. Day had begun to suspect that the time was right for baseball to return to New York City if a suitable location could be found. The Capitoline Grounds had been destroyed, however, and the Union of Morrisania's home in Tremont was scheduled for the same fate.[7] Day soon set his sites on the grounds of the Westchester Polo Club, located at the corner of 110th Street and Fifth Avenue. Fortunately, as a local paper later noted, "the Westchester Polo Club people found their expensive grounds, which were very little used for polo, quite an elephant on their hands, and they were glad to have Mr. Day help them out by leasing them for three days a week for business purposes."[8] Henry Chadwick declared it to be the first real enclosed professional grounds ever situated in New York City.[9]

An exhibition baseball game was first played on the polo grounds in September 1880. The results were encouraging enough that Day arranged for a professional club to play there in 1881 and 1882, though it remained unaffiliated with either the National League or its new rival, the American Association. After two years, he decided it was time to take the next step and acquired an exclusive lease on the polo grounds.[10] Polo required a much larger field than did baseball, and this fact gave Day an idea. Rather than choosing to join just one of the leagues, he took advantage of a newly signed peace agreement between the National League and the American Association and acquired franchises in both. To accommodate both clubs, he built two adjoining fields that were separated only by a canvas fence.

On a few occasions, the two teams' games were played simultaneously, which could lead to "bizarre scenes, with a National League center fielder crawling into the American Association outfield, recovering a ball, and then throwing it over the canvas fence back into his own path, and vice versa."[11] The southwest section of the Polo Grounds, as the baseball site officially came to be known, was occupied by the American Association's Metropolitans, and it had more serious problems than the southeast field. According to baseball historian Jerry Lansche, "The ground was uneven and stadium planners had used garbage as landfill, prompting pitcher Jack Lynch to say 'a player may go down for a grounder and come up with malaria.'"[12] Though Lansche may have confused this locale with the Metropolitans' next home, there is no question that the southwest diamond was ill suited for baseball. Some researchers believe that the Metropolitans began to use the southeast diamond on days when the National League club was not playing there.[13]

The Metropolitans' inferior location was a particularly vivid symbol of the increasingly apparent fact that the National League club was the owner's favorite. A pennant for the Metropolitans in 1884 did nothing to change this preference, and John Day responded to the triumph by arranging the transfer of two of the American Association club's best players—Tim Keefe and "Dude" Esterbrook—to his National League entry. (This dubious transaction was a precursor of the syndicate form of ownership that was reintroduced to baseball in the 1890s as a result of Day's financial woes.) After one season of sharing the Polo Grounds, the Metropolitans attempted to establish their own home base on a site near the East River between 107th and 109th streets. The club optimistically named its new field Metropolitan Park, but it was hard not to notice that the "park" was "covered with ash heaps and rubbish piles."[14] As a result, according to the *Brooklyn Eagle*, it soon became "known as 'The Dump' among the boys, as the ground is new made on an ash dumping field."[15] Another sportswriter observed that "the ground is filled in and the filling is of such a nature as to be decidedly unpleasant to the olfactory organs."[16]

Not only was the East River site unpleasant but the arrangements by which the Metropolitans retained its use were also among the shakiest in an era of impermanence. New York's board of aldermen had agreed to close 108th Street from Seventh Avenue to the East River to accommodate the ballpark. Unfortunately, the agreement could "be rescinded at any time and the new field broken up to grade the street whenever the new Board of Aldermen choose to decide that the street shall be reopened."[17] This state of affairs made it possible for the aldermen to "demand 'soap' or free tickets just as they choose in order to prevent the street—One Hundred and Eighth street—from being cut through, as it is only a temporarily withholding of the opening of that street to the river."[18] In an understatement, the *Brooklyn Eagle* observed that "To lay out money in constructing a new ground, with such control in the hands of men like New York Aldermen, is a waste of money."[19] Accommodations for the club were made with this uncertainty in mind. In a heavy wind, the flimsy outfield fence "went down like an eggshell" and was blown into the East River.[20] One smart-aleck reporter quipped that the team's manager "has not only had his fences chained to the ground, and big weights put in various parts of his field to keep his dump from being blown away, but has hired a corps of boatmen to go after the fence and bring it back every time it blows into the river."[21]

When the warm weather came, the smell emanating from the dump got worse, and it took plentiful doses of deodorizing compound just to make it bearable.[22] The Metropolitans soon elected to resume playing their home games on the National League club's diamond except when their schedules conflicted. The arrangement continued in 1885, but without Keefe and Esterbrook the club fell back to seventh place.

In December 1885, the Metropolitans were sold to Erastus Wiman, whose plans for the club bore some similarity to what John Cox Stevens had achieved with the Elysian Fields. Wiman was president of a Staten Island amusement park and also owned a ferry and railroad that transported people to Staten Island. His intention was to move the club to the St. George Cricket Grounds on Staten Island in order to give people another reason to visit his amusement park. He threw in a free round-trip ferry ride with every ticket to the ball game.[23]

The American Association was so appalled by this ploy that it ejected the Mets, but Wiman went to court and received an injunction.[24] As a result, after three years of playing second fiddle to Day's National League entry, the Metropolitans became second-class citizens at an amusement park. As the *Sporting News* noted, "The general opinion among base ball men is that the grounds at Staten Island as they are conducted at present are doomed to be a failure. The transportation is costly and anything but convenient. Mr. Wiman proposes to have other attractions, such as electric and pyrotechnic displays. The last may prove a drawing card."[25]

With the grandstand providing a beautiful view of the New York harbor and the construction of the Statue of Liberty, it soon seemed that the Mets' management wanted paying spectators to direct their gaze in any direction but the playing field! The situation grew worse in 1887 when Wiman built a large stage in right field for a production of a play called *The Fall of Babylon*, prompting the creation of a ground rule that any ball landing on the stage was a single. Following two lackluster seasons at the cricket grounds, the club disbanded.

The National League club, now known as the Giants, was the sole occupant of the Polo Grounds until 1888, at which point a familiar theme recurred. At the instigation of the Park Commission, New York's Board of Public Works announced plans to open 111th Street, meaning the fence around the Polo Grounds would have to be torn down. For nearly a year, Day made full use of his Tammany connections and kept the issue shuttling back and forth between the courts and legislatures. Then a judge ruled that the city's aldermen had violated the law by letting the club lease the grounds in the first place.[26] The New York state senate responded by passing a bill that would have allowed the Giants to keep their home, only to see it vetoed by the governor.[27] That sent the issue back to the aldermen, who had already been overridden once and now wanted no part of what had become a political hot potato. Hoping to "keep the friendship of the baseball capitalists without incurring the hostility of the property owners who want 111th street made ready to use," they went to farcical lengths to avoid having to take a vote.[28] While the politicians were straddling the fence, the ball club elected to take down its fence.[29]

Sportswriter Tim Murnane saw the saga as an example of the pettiness of New York municipal politics. He claimed in 1902 that "finding that Mr. Day would not stand for dictation the city fathers decided to cut a street through the polo grounds, forcing the New York club to the banks of the Harlem river. For the next ten years the crowds passing up to the new grounds could see the old polo grounds just as they were when the Giants used them, with no street cut through them and showing how little use there was for driving the ball club away from a popular grounds."[30] Day himself blamed the "grasping real estate men who have a pull in politics."[31] But the *New York Times* was more far-sighted in recognizing the situation as part of the recurrent pattern that had plagued ball clubs since the days of the Knickerbockers. The *Times* observed that any New York City club with a desirable location would inevitably "be crowded out of it within a few seasons by the demands of builders."[32]

Whoever was to blame, the defending National League champions were homeless as the 1889 season began. John B. Day initially opted to find temporary lodgings for the Giants. One factor in this decision was optimism that his political connections would enable him to return to the Polo Grounds.[33] But the determining factor in selecting the team's home was a familiar one—the complete lack of suitable land in Manhattan.[34] As a result, the Giants played two games in Jersey

City and then set up camp at the St. George Cricket Grounds, which had not been used for baseball since the Metropolitans disbanded. It was, to say the least, not an ideal setting. Wiman's stage still occupied part of right field, forcing the outfielders "to stand on this sloping platform," the *New York Times* noted. "The men will be provided with either rubber or heavily spiked shoes to travel over this incline."[35] This bizarre obstacle had an effect similar to the hills encountered in the early days of baseball, since "balls bound by the fielders with increased speed after they strike the wood work, and hits that would ordinarily prove good for two bases will yield home runs."[36] Matters were just as unsatisfactory for infielders. Balls skidded through the skin infield so rapidly and unpredictably that Cleveland second baseman Cub Stricker was said to be "afraid that every ball that comes near him will bound up and injure him."[37]

In addition, the benefits of proximity to the harbor were far outweighed by the practical disadvantages. The spring of 1889 saw the northeast deluged with rain, which resulted in the loss of twenty-two hundred lives in the Johnstown Flood. The consequences were far less catastrophic for the Giants, but they still proved a great nuisance. The grounds were virtually underwater by May.[38] The outfield soon resembled a giant "mud puddle," and the planks that were placed there did little to help the fielders who slid around in pursuit of balls.[39] At least the stage that had long tormented right fielders now provided a safe haven! By June, John Day had concluded that he would be unable to return the Giants to their old home and so leased a new site.

The location he selected was a plot of land known as the Lynch estate, which was situated in the north Harlem section of Manhattan, near 8th Avenue between 155th and 157th. Day had had his eye on the site since early April but had been thwarted by owner James J. Coogan's desire to sell rather than lease the property. Unwilling or unable to buy it himself, Day had gone so far as to put an ad in the New York papers offering to lease the grounds from any entrepreneur who would purchase them. He finally came to terms on a lease for about half of the area from Coogan on June 21.

In many ways, the site was unpromising. It was not until the 1860s that the city started laying streets north of 155th Street, meaning that the area that was to become the ballpark was still considered the outskirts of town. Moreover, until the early 1870s, Coogan's Hollow had been a wetland that was usually covered with water.[40] One contractor thought this was why Day had offered to lease the site: "That is low, marshy ground, and in case the company wanted to sell it for building purposes in a few years they would find they had a white elephant on their hands. That is the reason that a few weeks ago Mr. Day advertised for some persons to purchase that property, agreeing to pay $6000 a year rental for a five or ten years' lease."[41]

According to sportswriter Joe Vila, to make the field playable "It was necessary to fill in the swamps along the Harlem River with ashes taken from the elevated railroads, which at that time were operated with steam locomotive."[42] Even so, in the last game of the 1889 season Cap Anson hit a long drive that landed on an embankment in deep center field. The ball stuck there in the mud, and the slow-footed Anson rounded the bases while outfielder George Gore tried in vain to climb up the muddy hill to retrieve the ball.[43] Nonetheless, the site did have one major advantage in that elevated railroads ran past it, making it very accessible to fans. Perhaps even more importantly, John Day was in no position to be choosy, having acknowledged in April that there was "absolutely no suitable ground on the island for future seasons except this Lynch estate."[44]

The Giants played their first home game at Coogan's Hollow on July 8, 1889, in front of over ten thousand paying spectators and an estimated five thousand more watching from nearby "Dead-head Hill."[45] Although the park's infrastructure and the exact location of the playing field would change several times, this would remain the site at which New Yorkers would congregate to watch National League baseball until 1964. Another constant was that the old name of the Polo Grounds was retained, despite the fact that it is unclear whether polo had ever been played there.[46]

After the 1889 season, major league players formed a rival circuit and placed franchises in almost all the same cities as the National League. Nowhere was the challenge more direct than in New York, where one of the shareholders of the so-called Players' League entry was none other than James J. Coogan. The players' "Brotherhood" league selected the other half of Coogan's Hollow, which meant that for the second time in less than a decade, two major league teams from New York City would be playing on adjacent fields. The parks were so close together that fans in the right-field bleachers of the new park could watch the action in the Giants' park. In one early season game, the "World's Champions" flag in the National League park blew away and ended up in the new park.[47] In another, Mike Tiernan of the Giants hit a long home run that went clear out of the National League park and hit the fence of the Players' League park, earning him an ovation from both crowds.[48]

The problems of playing on a mud flat were particularly evident at the Players' League park. One early season game featured "a space of fifty feet square between second base and right field where the players sank up to their ankles in mud."[49] Another game was canceled altogether, and when play went ahead in the Giants' park, they were able to attract many of the fans who had turned out for the Players' League game.[50] With both leagues battling to survive, losing a gate to one's rivals was a significant setback.

The Players' League folded after a single season, leaving the Giants as the sole possessors of the Polo Grounds and New York City for the remainder of the decade. The club took advantage of the situation by reconfiguring its diamond's location to ensure the Giants would henceforth have Coogan's Bluff to themselves.

When the American League redefined itself as a major league in 1901, no initial effort was made to place a franchise in New York City. In addition to the harsh reality that almost no feasible sites existed for a ballpark, Giants owner Andrew Freedman had Tammany connections. It was thus taken for granted that he would use his political clout to have a street cut through any potential site.[51] The situation changed with the defeat of the Tammany slate in the 1901 elections.

American League president Ban Johnson had followed the campaign avidly and was reported to be "elated over the downfall of [Tammany leader Richard] Croker, as it means to him the loss of Freedman's power and political influence which has hitherto barred the entry of the American League into New York. Freedman so tied up the available grounds in New York that Johnson could not find room to put in a wedge."[52]

In 1903, the American League finally decided to place a rival club in Manhattan. The Giants still attempted to thwart them by buying up every potential site for a ball field, with McGraw claiming that he had "gone over Manhattan Island from the battery to the Harlem river very carefully and could not find a spot large enough to play a game of three old cat."[53] But the American League owners knew that they had a new weapon—dynamite, the use of which had been refined during the building of the railroads that now crisscrossed the country. They leased a lot in the Highlands (on the west side of Broadway between West 165th and West 168th streets) that was "nothing more or less than a rocky hill which had to be blasted and cut away before a level playing surface could be secured."[54] Extensive use of dynamite made the field ready for opening day, although there was still a gully in the outfield.[55] During its stay at this site, the club that eventually became known as the Yankees was generally referred to as the Highlanders in honor of the location.

Although dynamite opened new terrains for ballparks, it didn't eliminate the familiar problem that had long haunted urban baseball. In 1911 the club's landlords, the New York Institute for the Blind, decided that the property was too valuable and evicted the team. The team's owners had anticipated this action and by then had been looking seriously for a new ballpark for two years. But once again they were thwarted by the shortage of land in Manhattan. The options were so limited that the club even considered a ballpark that would float on the Harlem River.[56] Work was eventually begun at 225th and Broadway, but soon abandoned due to myriad problems, one of them being a creek that ran past the site.[57] The result was that, from 1913 until the opening of Yankee Stadium in 1923, the two major league clubs in the nation's largest and wealthiest city shared the former mud flat in Coogan's Hollow.

These years saw the emergence of a number of aspirants to major-league status that cast wistful glances toward New York, only to conclude that establishing a franchise there was impracticable. One of the principals of the short-lived United States League echoed a familiar theme in 1912 when he claimed that he had gone "over the maps of the city with a microscope and couldn't find a place suitable for a ball park." He turned down the only locations he was offered because he "wanted a regular field where the players could make something more than a single."[58] This description makes one wonder what the rules of the "New York" version of baseball would have looked like if the game had emerged after the 1840s!

This drastic scarcity of appropriate land put New York baseball clubs in a unique situation. The combination of their status as tenants and the constant risk of fire to wooden structures meant that most turn-of-the-century clubs still looked at their ballparks as short-term homes and treated them as such. But when John T. Brush bought the Giants from Freedman in 1903, he understood that he did not have the option of moving and behaved accordingly.

As early as 1905, Brush was demonstrating his long-term commitment to the Polo Grounds by discussing his plans to use the entire Coogan's Hollow for a stadium that would seat fifty thousand spectators.[59] Soon, he was talking openly about building the first all-steel baseball stadium.[60] He became convinced that a clean, appealing stadium was key to competing with the nearby Highlanders and, with his Giants reaping large profits, spared no expense.[61] One of those expenditures was paying top dollar for a groundskeeper whose work Brush was familiar with from their days together in Indianapolis: John Murphy.

1. Tom Murphy (center) flanked by four of the future Hall of Famers who played for the great Orioles teams of the 1890s: left to right, Wee Willie Keeler, Hughey Jennings, Joe Kelley, and John McGraw. National Baseball Hall of Fame Library, Cooperstown, New York.

2. National Commission chairman and Reds owner Garry Herrmann (left) and Pirates owner Barney Dreyfuss (right) were two of baseball's most influential figures in the early twentieth century. Dreyfuss had a love-hate relationship with his groundskeeper, John Murphy, finding that he couldn't work with Murphy but that his low-lying ballpark couldn't remain playable without him. Library of Congress, LC-DIG-ggbain-04424.

3. John McGraw (left, as Giants manager) and Wilbert Robinson (right, as Dodgers manager) were two of the leaders of the Orioles of the 1890s, the club that challenged baseball's conventions so relentlessly that Johnny Ward is said to have marveled: "This isn't baseball the Orioles are playing. It's a whole new game." McGraw's and Robinson's careers were intertwined with those of both Murphy brothers. Library of Congress, LC-DIG-ggbain-16227.

4. The charismatic Hughey Jennings was one of the leaders of the Orioles when Tom Murphy was their groundskeeper, and brought him back to the major leagues with Detroit in 1909 after Tom's release from prison. Library of Congress, LC-DIG-ggbain-16448.

5. The fire that leveled the Polo Grounds at the start of the 1911 season seemed a devastating blow, but in many ways it proved to be a blessing in disguise for the club. Library of Congress, LC-USZ62-80748.

6. The Polo Grounds at the start of the 1913 season, when the ballpark became home to both the Giants and the American League club that had generally been referred to as the Highlanders. But having left its home on the Highlands, the team needed a new name and gradually became known as the Yankees. Library of Congress, LC-DIG-ggbain-13274.

7. The Polo Grounds grass that John Murphy tended with such care at the opening game of the 1912 World Series. The Giants lost the Series in heartbreaking fashion by blowing a lead in the tenth inning of the deciding game. Library of Congress, LC-DIG-ggbain-14449.

8. Overflow crowds such as this one at the Polo Grounds meant that fans sat on the field of play, which necessitated special ground rules. Library of Congress, LC-DIG-ggbain-02322.

9. American League Ban Johnson, who brashly took on the National League in 1901, flanked by some of the league's owners and front office members, including Charles Comiskey of the White Sox. Left to right, top: Frank J. Navin, Ben S. Minor, and Frank Farrell; bottom: Charles Comiskey, Ban Johnson, and Joseph J. Lannin. Library of Congress, LC-DIG-ggbain-17210.

10. Athletics' manager Connie Mack hired Tom Murphy in 1901, but the choice proved ill fated: Murphy ended up in prison for a near-fatal attack on Mack's brother. The following year, Mack spotted the fugitive Murphy and had him arrested. Library of Congress, LC-DIG-ggbain-09862.

11. Pioneer concessionaire Harry Stevens (left) with National Commission chairman Garry Herrmann. Stevens was one of the many men who made the Polo Grounds a special place during John Murphy's tenure, popularizing the hot dog, for example, and generally bringing ballpark concessions to a new level. He lost his entire inventory in the 1911 fire but bounced back quickly. Library of Congress, LC-DIG-ggbain-14970.

12. Jim Thorpe of the Giants at Emerson Field in Marlin Springs, Texas, which John Murphy worked tirelessly to prepare for spring training each year. The identity of the man in the background holding the broom is not known, but it may just be our only glimpse of John Murphy. If so, it would be appropriate that he is in the background. Library of Congress, LC-DIG-ggbain-50300.

13. Boston's Fenway Park is one of the last of the first wave of steel-and-concrete stadiums still in use. Library of Congress, LC-USZ62-103058.

14. When Ebbets Field first opened, there seemed to be plenty of room for fans to park. But that would change. Library of Congress, LC-DIG-ggbain-22423.

15. The American League was able to place a team in New York in 1903 through considerable cunning. They bought a lot in the Highlands that was "nothing more or less than a rocky hill which had to be blasted and cut away before a level playing surface could be secured." As shown by this 1908 photo, with a lot of help from dynamite, they succeeded in making it playable. Library of Congress, LC-DIG-ggbain-00316.

16. John T. Brush gave John Murphy his first National League groundskeeping position with Indianapolis in 1888. Fifteen years later, Brush was the owner of the Giants and hired Murphy to oversee the former mud flat known as the Polo Grounds. Library of Congress, LC-DIG-ggbain-09870.

17. Patrick Murphy's gravestone at Indianapolis's Crown Hill Cemetery. Courtesy of W. C. Madden.

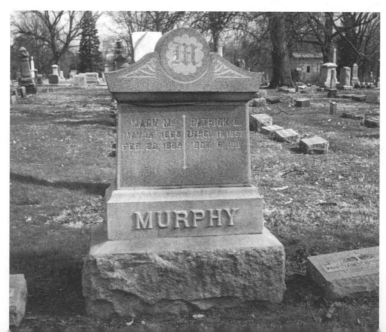

9. John Murphy of the Polo Grounds

All the factors discussed in chapter 8 made working at the Polo Grounds the ultimate challenge for a groundskeeper but also a dream job for a talented one. Every indication suggests that John Murphy reveled in the new opportunity.

After the 1905 season, he replaced the ugly cinder path behind the outfield ropes with flower beds similar to those he had introduced in Baltimore.[1] In the years that followed, he would continue adding new touches until even normally hard-boiled sportswriters were moved by the picturesque vision thus created:

> His eye for beauty and love of nature is well known by every patron of the Polo Grounds who has seen old rain barrels cut in two, painted in bright colors, and made into portable flower beds in which geraniums bloom during the baseball season, to decorate the lawn in front of the field boxes. Murphy can't make the turf at the Polo Grounds talk, but he has trained the grass so well on either side of the home plate that the words "New York" and "Visitors" stand out in conspicuous fashion on the velvety lawn of the ball park.[2]

Another added,

> There is as much difference in the landscape presented by different major league ball fields as there is between the

well-kept lawn of a millionaire and the scraggy looking turf in front of the average flat building in Chicago. Patrons of the Polo grounds in New York and the Forbes field in Pittsburgh are given part of the value of their money in the pleasing outlook from the stands. A perfectly kept field of bright green, level as a billiard table, and broken only by the necessary base lines, is an attractive sight in itself. Flowers around the inside of the stands add their beauty to the Polo grounds picture.[3]

The Polo Grounds required unstinting care, and John Murphy was, as usual, up to the challenge. As sportswriter Harry Dix Cole observed in 1912,

There is one person at least for whom the base ball season lasts all year round, and that is Groundkeeper Murphy. Ever since the season closed he has been as busy as can be grooming his pet, the Brush Stadium, for next year's campaign. That portion of the field between the diamond and the grandstand had been raised and resodded, and has a regular May gleam. He has filled in the ground along the foul line behind first base and it is now quite hard and firm. The outfield in right centre and also deep centre has been resodded, while the base lines have all been massaged with a brand of earth especially imported by the industrious caretaker.[4]

When Napoleon Lajoie played at the Polo Grounds for the first time he remarked, "I'd like to play here all the time. If a fellow doesn't get the ball it is his fault. The old pill comes true as a die every clip."[5] Quite a contrast to Tom Murphy's work at Union Park! Lajoie's judgment seems to have been universal: "Visiting players always commented favorably on the level and true condition of the Polo infield, and every American League visitor [in the summer the Yankees moved there] was enthusiastic about it."[6] Ballplayer-turned-sportswriter Sam Crane added this endorsement:

Groundkeeper Murphy has a national reputation in his own particular line, and fully deserves the name he has as being the best ground keeper in the country. . . . The Polo Grounds are justly celebrated. To one who has visited the grass burned fields of the ball parks in the West, to see the Giants' home grounds in their present magnificent condition is a revelation. One wonders how Murphy can keep the field in such superb shape. The turf is as close and firm and smooth as the best cricket fields in England, the country that is famous for its well-kept lawns "How does Murphy do it?" is the question always asked by visiting players. . . . The Polo Grounds are the model baseball grounds of the country, and are so acknowledged by every player who has been fortunate enough to play on them. They are an artistic dream.[7]

John Murphy didn't settle for just making the Polo Grounds turf "as springy as a velvet carpet and as smooth as a billiard table," however.[8] As he had done in Baltimore, he demonstrated through his own distinctive touches that he was not merely a caretaker but a landscape gardener. Regulars at the Polo Grounds soon became aware that Murphy's "chief delight is in evolving new and unique patterns on the grass around home plate and on the coaching lines, and the fans never fail to show their appreciation of such work at the opening of each season."[9] And Murphy never disappointed them, always finding time amidst his labors for signature flourishes while undertaking at least one new project each season. During the 1908 season, for example, he patterned the grass in the first-base coaching box so it formed the word STOP.[10] Sam Crane observed in 1910 that "Murphy's most striking effort this season was in covering the grass-bare spaces back of the diamond with a layer of black dirt, almost inky black in color, and not only does that furnish a pleasant color comparison with the rest of the diamond, but it allows no dust even on the windiest of days. What the new layer is Murphy refuses to divulge. It is a secret of his own."[11]

Over sixty years later, sportswriter Fred Lieb recalled that one of the features of opening day in 1911 was that "Irish John Murphy, the grounds keeper, had stuck into the ground old Irish flags with the gold harp on a field of green at the positions played by captain and second baseman, Larry Doyle, and the redheaded right fielder, Red Jack Murray."[12] The next season, fans were greeted by another decorative addition: "John Murphy, the Polo Grounds ground keeper and the most artistic of all the baseball landscape architects," the *New York Sun* reported, "has a new wrinkle for patrons when the Giants return. A baseball has been reproduced on the grass, showing seams, trademark and everything except the cork centre."[13]

As these efforts suggest, John Murphy's years at the Polo Grounds saw his disposition grow steadily sunnier. On December 7, 1911, he married Mary Agnes Hunt in Indianapolis, and this no doubt contributed to his mellowing from a sometimes angry young man into a distinguished elder statesman of the profession. His range of interests broadened to include an Irish setter that he proudly entered in dog shows.[14] Although he and Mary Agnes married too late in life to have children, his earlier nicknames of "Red" and "Jack" began to be replaced with the affectionate "Pop."

Playing no small part in this mellowing was the fact that John Murphy's skill was finally earning him the respect he had long craved. Even visiting reporters like the *Chicago Tribune*'s "Sy" Sanborn hailed him as holding "the world's championship among baseball landscape gardeners."[15] Murphy was increasingly able to rely on the luxury of hiring a small staff during busy periods to help him with the more arduous tasks. He must have appreciated both the help itself and the symbolic acknowledgment that groundskeeping was a profession. Just as important, Murphy's skill was finally earning him financial recognition. Before the 1906 season, he signed a two-year contract to remain groundskeeper of the Polo Grounds.[16] Several years later, it was reported that "His salary as groundkeeper for the Giants was larger than that of most players outside the major leagues."[17]

There is no record of exactly how much John Murphy was paid. We can be sure that it was not a phenomenal sum, since even top players were not wealthy men in this era, and most groundskeepers barely made enough to scrape by on. It was customary to pay them only during the season, and, as noted earlier, some minor league clubs cut checks to the groundskeeper only when the club was in town. Most likely, Murphy's salary was in the range of the annual $3,000 that his successor, Henry Fabian, received.[18] More important than the exact amount is that the remuneration seems to have been enough to keep Murphy happy. Perhaps the knowledge that he sat atop the pay scale of his profession was the key. It could have been small perks like the two-year contract and the regular gifts from players that made the difference. Possibly the crucial factor was the security of knowing that the Giants would not disband as so many of his minor league employers had. Or maybe it was just the mellowing effect of age and marriage. In any event, during Murphy's years at the Polo Grounds, there are no signs of the dissatisfaction with salary that had been a recurring issue in his previous stops.

Finally secure in the knowledge that his expertise was recognized, John Murphy became a sort of roving ambassador for baseball landscape gardening. He came to be "regarded the most expert baseball groundkeeper in the country," the *New York Times* observed, "and because of his expert knowledge and years of experience groundkeepers from all over the country frequently came to consult 'Pop.'"[19] By 1910, Murphy's services were "in demand all over the National and American League circuits, and also by college managements, who want their baseball diamonds and the gridirons put in as perfect condition as human handiwork can make them."[20]

Murphy remained the acknowledged master on drainage issues and was frequently called in to supervise the opening of new fields. Millionaire owner Morton F. Plant brought Murphy in to oversee the opening of Plant Field in New London, Connecticut, and the "result was a diamond flat that was perfection. It was wonderfully drained and shed water after a rain like a duck."[21] Another consultation enabled Murphy to return to Erie to supervise the installation of a new field.[22] Even Frank Chance, the manager of the hated Cubs, was so impressed by the new soil that Murphy introduced behind the plate in 1910 that he "ordered two car-loads of it from Murphy to be sent to the Chicago ball grounds."[23]

Although the distinguishing elements of John Murphy's handiwork were very different from those of his brother Tom, he was not above scheming with John McGraw to make the Polo Grounds favor the Giants. Neutral hitting backgrounds in outfield areas had been around since at least 1894, when batters at Cincinnati's League Park complained that advertisements in center field were preventing them from focusing on pitched balls. In response, park superintendent John Schwab created a deep green backdrop in center field.[24] Some clubs followed suit but not all, and by the twentieth century the proliferation of colorful advertising signs was causing problems for hitters. To take advantage of this, pitchers would "shift from side to side in the slab to make the ball come to the batter on a line with some blinding sign," Johnny Evers and Hugh Fullerton explained. "The batters, being in the majority on each team, however, insist upon good solid green backgrounds to increase hitting, and overrule the pitchers, who prefer glaring yellow, or white, or a motley of colors."[25] Several beanings and lobbying by David Fultz, head of the Players' Fraternity (another attempt at a union), prompted the major leagues to mandate a blank green wall in center field in 1914, but in the meantime a lot of chicanery had taken place.[26]

McGraw and Murphy found a unique way to exploit this issue. The Giants had a crew of mediocre defensive outfielders in 1909, so when new stands were built "McGraw ordered them painted a washed yellow, a bilious-hued, glaring, eye-racking yellow," in the words of Evers and Fullerton. "The background offered by the stand was a desperate one against which to field, but McGraw had the satisfaction of knowing that the other fellows, no matter how superior mechanically, could not derive much satisfaction from their superiority in that field."[27] As he had done in Pittsburgh and Baltimore, John Murphy borrowed one of his brother's old tricks in 1906: "The claim is made that the dirt around the plate at the Polo Grounds is mixed with a greasy or soapy substance that causes the bat to slip out of the batters' hands if they rub their hands in it. The same dirt is also around the pitcher's slab also [sic] to make the ball hard to hold."[28]

Led by McGraw and the standout pitching of Christy Mathewson and "Iron Man" Joe McGinnity, the Giants rang up pennants in 1904 and 1905 and three more between 1911 and 1913. The additional pennants meant that the brothers Murphy had prepared the fields of twelve National League pennant winners in a twenty-year span. Despite the success, the Giants were a club that often seemed cursed. In 1908, the Giants seemed headed for a pennant until an apparent victory against the archrival Chicago Cubs was overturned. The Cubs appealed that rookie Fred Merkle had run off the field after what seemed to be the game-winning hit without touching second base, and while fans mobbed the field, they successfully claimed a run-negating force out. Eventually, umpire Hank O'Day sided with them, and so did National League president Harry Pulliam. When the two clubs ended the season in a dead heat, the disputed game was replayed at the Polo Grounds, and the Cubs prevailed.

Four years after enduring this agonizing loss of the pennant, the Giants found an equally heartbreaking way to lose the 1912 World Series. With the Giants and Boston Red Sox each having won three games apiece (along with one tie), the deciding game went to extra innings. In the top of the tenth, New York scored a single run on a clutch hit by Fred Merkle. Giant ace Christy Mathewson returned to the mound in the bottom half, needing just three outs to make the Giants world champions and bring redemption to Merkle. He never got them. Instead, outfielder Fred Snodgrass dropped a routine fly ball to start the bottom of the tenth. Snodgrass made amends by making a spectacular catch on the next batter, but that would be forgotten. The Giants gave the Red Sox another extra out on a foul fly that Merkle could have caught. Instead, Mathewson called for catcher Chief Meyers to take the ball, and it fell harmlessly to the ground. The Red Sox capitalized by scoring two runs to win the series and, just as unfairly, "Snodgrass's Muff" took its place alongside "Merkle's Boner."

Through these adversities, the Giants seem to have become a closer group, and their leader softened, as much as it was possible for him to do so. John McGraw never stopped agonizing over every defeat, however. He was especially bitter over Pulliam's decision on the Merkle force out because the National League president was a protégé of Barney Dreyfuss, and McGraw viewed the ruling as spite. Yet the combative manager stood resolutely by Merkle and Snodgrass through their ordeals. Defeat thus did what triumphs could never do by showing that there was a noble and even charming side to this most hard-bitten of competitors.

The Polo Grounds, under John Murphy's influence, was beginning to undergo a similar metamorphosis. Gradually, it gained acceptance as the home of the Giants and, like any home, its idiosyncrasies came to be recognized as the heart of its charm. Bizarre features that reflected the proximity of the Harlem River, such as the stadium's horseshoe shape and the overhang in left field, simply added to its appeal. So did trying to watch the game from Coogan's Bluff, where, as one observer later recalled, only a handful of players were visible: "you got to see the shortstop, the left fielder, and the center fielder. You saw the second baseman on plays near the base and the third baseman on plays away from it."[29] Perhaps the appeal of this peculiar activity derived from the knowledge that the pillars inside the stadium ensured that many paying spectators had scarcely better views.

Although John McGraw, John Murphy, and the Polo Grounds all underwent a mellowing process, the job of tending the stadium was far from free of challenges. This was just as well because if there was one thing John Murphy seems to have craved even more than respect, it was a challenge. The fact that the Polo Grounds had been built on a mud flat created by the Harlem River lent it charm for many, but for John Murphy it produced all-too-familiar flooding problems.[30] The *Sporting News* later noted that Murphy "used to keep a rowboat and on days when the Harlem swelled and the Polo Grounds was covered with surface water, Murphy would get out his oars, paddle around in the outfield and find the manholes which answered for a drainage system."[31]

John Murphy's ability to deal with the Polo Grounds' drainage problems is easy to take for granted. To fully appreciate his talent, it is necessary to consider what happened when he wasn't on hand. A Giants game there in 1901, before either of Murphy's tenures, had to be canceled, the *Brooklyn Eagle* noted, because "The diamond with the exception of third base, was in fair condition, but out in right field the water was a foot deep and it would have been dangerous to have forced any player to wallow about in that territory. Willie Keeler, when he looked over the ground in that section of the field, remarked that he was not up on water polo, but if management insisted, he would build a raft and take his chances."[32] A couple of weeks later, another deluge came, and the grounds "were turned into a good-sized lake, and they were still submerged at the east end last evening, there being a couple of feet of water near the Eighth Avenue entrance."[33]

The Columbia University football team tried to play home games at the Polo Grounds, with similarly unsatisfactory results. Heavy rains before a 1903 game against Williams College left parts of the field covered in as much as three feet of water. A rowboat had to be used to convey the officials to the part of the field that wasn't submerged. The officials improvised a new, smaller playing area in the playable part of the field, while fans grumbled that the forty-five-minute delay would not have been necessary if the new field had been mapped out that morning. Even on the reduced field, slipping and fumbling were frequent. An extra point was not attempted after the game's lone touchdown because the ball would have landed in the water, while two punts landed in the water and the action stopped while they were gingerly retrieved.[34]

Floods did not cease at the Polo Grounds when John Murphy was installed there, but fans never had cause to complain that an unplayable field was the result of lack of foresight on his part. Meanwhile, new challenges continually arose. The most heartbreaking one must have come in the early morning hours of April 14, 1911, when fire destroyed much of the Polo Grounds. Reports about John Murphy's whereabouts when the blaze broke out conflicted. Most newspaper accounts reported only the presence of park custodian John F. Higgins, but the *New York Herald* credited Murphy with rescuing six English pointers that he housed in the clubhouse.[35] When the ballpark reopened, the *New York Times* noted cryptically, "Ground Keeper Murphy saved the diamond from the fire. The grass is as velvety as ever and emerald green."[36] This may imply that Murphy was on hand when the fire occurred, but it could simply be a reporter's little joke about Murphy's single-mindedness.

The blaze was a tragedy for many, including Giants concessionaire Harry Stevens, who lost most of his inventory. But for the Giants it proved in many ways a blessing in disguise. Their American League rivals volunteered to let the Giants share their ballpark, ending the longstanding animosity between the clubs. The fire also allowed John T. Brush to negotiate a long-term lease on the Polo Grounds and then carry through his desire to build a concrete-and-steel edifice beneath Coogan's Bluff. The new structure was begun immediately and was ready for play only eleven weeks after the fire. Brush announced that the Giants' home would henceforth be known as Brush Stadium, which would have made it the first ballpark to be known as a stadium. But the name didn't catch on, as the public was too accustomed to using the familiar name of Polo Grounds.

Other challenges for John Murphy were less catastrophic. One spring, some of the Giant players planted cabbages and onions in the midst of Murphy's prized flower beds. "The results tickled them and surprised the groundkeeper," sportswriter I. E. Sanborn reported, "for in among the sweet posies various sturdy plants of plebeian origin and type appeared, and he tackled the seed merchant about it in anger at the imposition."[37] There were other occasional reminders that Murphy's temper could return when he felt his territory was being trespassed upon. After the 1908 season, for example, he quarreled bitterly with the builder who was working on a new grandstand, and went home to Pittsburgh. Only McGraw's intercession convinced Murphy to return.[38] The indefatigable Irishman also found time to wrestle with a problem that horticulturalists are still working on today. After the 1911 season, he was approached by two colleges and asked to build a real-grass indoor field for them to play on during the winter. Murphy threw himself into the project with customary vigor, although the ultimate results are unknown.[39]

The 1913 season brought yet another new challenge for John Murphy. The Giants' American League rivals began to share the Polo Grounds with the Giants, in what was expected to be a short-term arrangement. (And, since they no longer played in the Highlands, the club's old nickname gave way to a new one: the Yankees.) The arrangement brought inconvenience to many, but none felt the hardship more keenly than Murphy. A visiting reporter noted a difference at the Polo Grounds: "The roses and posies were the same, or similar, but the playing field lacked its old-time gloss, and its green was spotted." When he asked John Murphy about it, "the groundkeeper growled his alibi in no uncertain language. That dod-swatted arrangement whereby the Giants share their plant with the New York American League team for this season is responsible for the change in the looks of the playing field." The writer then explained:

One of the teams is home all the time, and [Yankees] Manager [Frank] Chance in particular is a bear for morning practices. He has the Yankees out early every possible day at home. Manager McGraw is almost equally insistent on morning practice, but starts it later. In the afternoon there is a game every day except Sunday, unless it rains, and his men can't work in the rain to any advantage, and won't work on Sundays without double pay or better. The only chances Murphy and his crew have had to manicure the playing field since the season opened were early in the morning, at lunch time, and after the game.[40]

It is perhaps just as well that Murphy would not be around to see the joint occupancy of the Polo Grounds become a decade-long arrangement. And it is certainly a blessing that it was his able successor,

Henry Fabian, who had to endure such indignities as the trampling of the Polo Grounds' grass by soccer players as well as by elephants from Paine's fireworks show (which also left rockets embedded in the turf), or the dynamite blasting by subway workers that unsettled the outfield. Perhaps the worst offenders were the college football fans who tore down the goalposts after games, causing Fabian to rant: "Them educated fellas is vandalous. And besides they ain't got a single, solitary grain of respect."[41] John Murphy would most certainly have agreed.

10. Marlin Springs

Though the Polo Grounds became John Murphy's home, in his years as its groundskeeper he also established a home away from home. That site was the diamond at the Giants' spring training camp in Marlin Springs, Texas, a spa town noted for its baths and springs. Its arid climate had two additional recommendations: it was ideal for helping players get into shape and also ensured that games would not be postponed by poor weather. Because of these benefits, when the Giants arrived in Marlin Springs in 1908 they were hardly the first team to have conceived of using it and the larger adjacent town of Marlin as a preseason base. The first occupant had been the Chicago White Sox in 1904 following the recommendation of garrulous baseball man and raconteur Ted Sullivan.

Sullivan had proclaimed with his typical infectious enthusiasm, "If I had looked the United States over for a spring training ground for a ball club, I do not believe I could have found a spot I would pick ahead of Marlin Springs." He claimed that he had heard about it from a rheumatic so transformed by the climate that he had left his crutches behind. Sullivan waxed eloquent about the hotel's "beautiful natatorium equipped with hot sulphur and all kinds of baths, with attendants ready to make the cripple walk and the dyspeptic eat." To top matters off, the ball field was on level ground a mere four blocks from the hotel. Sullivan made the locale sound too good to be true.[1]

Unfortunately, like many of Ted Sullivan's stories, his account was apparently too good to be true. (For example, the hotel where the Giants stayed was actually two miles from the ball field, although it's possible that Sullivan was referring to a different hotel.) The White Sox were succeeded in using Marlin Springs as a training site by the Cardinals in 1905 and the Reds in 1907.[2] The fact that none of these clubs remained long suggests that each had decided that the grass was greener elsewhere. Once again this is a metaphor that has both a figurative and a literal component, for the same climate that offered so many advantages also made it very difficult to maintain a suitable playing field.

John McGraw, however, knew that he had a secret weapon. When he announced in December 1907 that the Giants would train in Marlin Springs in 1908, he explained that he would arrive with the rookies around February 20. The veteran players would follow on March 1. Preceding all of them would be John Murphy, who would arrive on February 1 to prepare Emerson Field.[3] When the Giants began to arrive on the nineteenth, an excited Murphy greeted them and accurately predicted that Marlin Springs would prove a great town for training camp. He added: "It's lucky they sent me down ahead, for the grounds had been given up to steers, stray pigs and horses, so I had my work laid out to fix things right." Murphy reported that the grounds were now "as level as a billiard table," although even he could only do so much in three weeks—the field remained a bit sandy and the grass sparse.[4]

Predictably, Murphy had soon addressed this issue as well, and it became an annual ritual for the groundskeeper to precede the Giants to Marlin Springs. At first, John McGraw would send Murphy south a month or so before the players, but soon Murphy was beginning his work in December.[5] Without fail, he "transformed the field of trees and stones into a smooth diamond, and made it one of the best training grounds in that section of the country. . . . Murphy can make grass grow on the bald spots of a baseball diamond faster than any groundkeeper in captivity," the *New York Times* declared.[6] His success with Emerson Field affected much more than just that small patch of ground. It also became yet another way in which the Murphy brothers helped to reconfigure the contours of the game.

The origins of Southern spring training camps are another chapter of baseball history that has been oversimplified because the initial practical obstacles have faded from memory. For example, it has sometimes been claimed that such camps sprang from the imagination of some innovative soul in the late 1880s. Nothing could be further from the truth. Early clubs were acutely aware that a trip through the South would be a wonderful way to prepare for the season, and there were several notable efforts. The Red Stockings of Cincinnati and the White Stockings of Chicago both traveled to New Orleans in April 1870 to play exhibition games and round themselves into shape. In 1871, the Mutuals of New York went to Savannah, Georgia, to work the players into condition, and six years later, the Indianapolis club in the League Alliance conducted a preseason tour that started in Texas and continued to New Orleans, Memphis, and St. Louis.[7]

Such tours represented a tremendous financial risk, however, and any number of obstacles had to be overcome. One of the most daunting was that baseball enthusiasm in the South lagged far behind the rest of the country. When Frank Bancroft tried to arrange a stop in Montgomery, Alabama, in 1880, he received a firm "no" and this discouraging explanation from his Southern correspondent: "Several reasons might be assigned for this opinion of mine, but the first one is likely to be conclusive: we have no local club. For that matter we have no ball ground, and a personal experience justifies me in saying that our people have never shown the slightest enthusiasm over baseball as a fine art. You might get your work in quite profitably selling corn solvents or worm medicines; tame Indians, dressed simply in scalping knives and brass band, have been successful lately as advertising mediums, but shows requiring tickets are not looked upon with favor."[8]

In addition, with the Civil War still a recent and bitter memory, Southerners in communities that had baseball teams did not go out of their way to invite tours by "Yankee" clubs. This fact in turn increased the risk entailed by enterprising clubs and the amount of planning needed to pull off a successful Southern tour. It is easy to understand why many clubs that would have liked to begin the season with a Southern tour ended up staying closer to home.

By the 1890s, conditions were becoming more favorable, however. The South was warming to baseball, and Southern spring training trips became more common. Brooklyn pitcher Ed Stein offered the following comment in 1896: "I think a Southern trip is almost necessary on account of the warm weather. In the North it remains quite cold during the whole of March and outside practice would be almost impossible. The season starts so early that the players could hardly get in shape in time for practicing here."[9] As Stein suggested, such trips were coming to be perceived as a competitive requirement that no club felt they could do without. By the early twentieth century Southern training camps were virtually standard, but finding adequate sites continued to be difficult. The Arkansas spa town of Hot Springs was a popular locale for several years, but clubs began to leave because the Pirates had an exclusive lease on "the only piece of ground in or near the town that is laid out for baseball."[10]

Clubs began setting their sights on even more southerly locations, but that led to the challenge of finding spots where grass could be grown. Many clubs made do with "skin infields," which were devoid of grass and through which balls scooted. Infielders complained bitterly that skin infields were better suited for target practice than infield practice. A more serious concern was that, according to respected baseball men like Arthur Irwin, young players who learned to play on skin diamonds were unable to make the transition to grass.[11] Unfortunately, there were no shortcuts to the cultivation of grass in such climates. Only a skilled and experienced groundskeeper could do so, as clubs found to their chagrin. Before the 1909 season, ballplayer Jack Warner worked long and hard to create a grassy infield at Athletic Park in Galveston, Texas. The yield was so meager that he reversed course and made a skin diamond instead.[12]

The year after he dismissed John Murphy, Pirates owner Barney Dreyfuss tried sending "his ground keeper from Pittsburg to Hot

Springs just to put in order the practice grounds in the latter place," the *Sporting Life* noted. This approach was so novel that the correspondent who reported it asked rhetorically, "Did one ever hear of another club doing a thing like that?"[13] The difficulty with this approach was that it meant added expenses and risked hindering the groundskeeper from preparing the home park for the season. The result, as sportswriter Joe S. Jackson remarked during the 1909 preseason, was that "a majority of the diamonds down this way, outside of the Southern league, are skinned."[14]

Because of these problems, it became customary for clubs to choose a new site for spring practice each year in a continuing effort to find greener pastures. In 1899, a *Sporting Life* correspondent observed that "Considering the number of years base ball teams have gone South, it seems strange that no club has yet selected a permanent place for spring practice. They wander around from one place to another down South like the Ponce de Leon looking for the fountain of eternal youth . . . it is a rare occurrence for a team to train two successive seasons at the same place."[15] As late as 1912, Connie Mack admitted that "I can't say that I have ever found a place where everything is perfect. I guess our record will show that we have never gone to the same place two years in succession."[16]

John Murphy's expertise helped to change that. As one of his obituaries would later note: "One of his accomplishments was to make a really good field of the practice grounds at Marlin, Texas."[17] This feat enabled the Giants to come back to Marlin Springs year after year and more generally helped boost baseball in the South. Until Murphy paved the way, a vicious cycle had plagued spring training sites. Since playing conditions were poor, teams changed sites almost every year, and many deserted their home base early to tour. This impermanence in turn meant that towns had little incentive to invest in better facilities.

Once Murphy's handiwork in Marlin Springs showed Southern communities that clubs would return annually to a nice facility, they became willing to accommodate them. As Sid Mercer explained in 1910: "The establishment of permanent base ball training camps in the South by the New York and Pittsburg clubs of the National League and the advantages of holding preliminary practices on fields laid out to conform to big league standards is paving the way for a system of splendidly equipped base ball plants in Dixie."[18] Johnny Evers and Hugh S. Fullerton confirmed in 1912 that the trend was "more and more toward permanent training camps, and against exhibition tours." They explained that this course had the important benefit of allowing clubs the option of "operating their training plants all winter and sending the young player drafted or purchased there early in the winter to develop under the eye of an experienced coach, who will turn them over to the manager ready for play."[19]

Marlin Springs was the training camp for the Giants from 1908 until 1918, longer than any other previous club had stayed in one location for spring training.[20] The residents of Marlin showed their appreciation to Murphy by presenting him with numerous gifts, including an Elk's emblem, a cowboy suit, and a big Texas hat.[21]

11. The Later Years

Details about the later years of the Murphy brothers have proved to be especially elusive. Tom Murphy's prison sentence was scheduled to run until June 1905, but he must have either been released early for good behavior or received credit for time spent in jail while awaiting trial because he was back in baseball in the spring of 1905. Sportswriter J. Ed Grillo, who had been hired as president of the Toledo entry in the American Association, decided that spring that the quickest way to attract fans was to make Toledo's Armory Park more attractive. He hired Tom Murphy, who quickly had the park looking like "a revelation in every way," according to a *Sporting Life* correspondent. Among the groundskeeper's innovations was "the placing of the home and visitors' benches below the surface several feet. The benches are covered and quite up to date, as only in the big leagues."[1]

Nevertheless, after a single season word came that "Tom Murphy, the best groundkeeper Toledo ever had, has resigned and left for his home in Indianapolis."[2] The following spring he was reportedly "drawing some $1,500 per as superintendent of the Nashville track."[3] After that, his whereabouts become increasingly difficult to trace. During the 1909 season, he joined Detroit and Hugh Jennings, another old friend from his Baltimore days. Detroit won three straight American League pennants from 1907 to 1909, which raises several intriguing questions. One would love, for example, to know how Murphy got along with the ultracompetitive Ty Cobb. Even more fascinating is the question of how Connie Mack reacted to the return to the American

League of the man who had nearly killed his brother. Jennings's Tigers and Mack's Athletics were already bitter rivals, and Tom Murphy's presence can only have heightened the tense feelings as the two teams battled it out in another tight pennant race in 1909. Unfortunately, the details are lost to history.

Tom Murphy may have played a role in one of his nephews earning a trial with the Tigers. Frank W. Dunn, son of Tom's eldest sister Mary, was a pitching prospect. Family tradition asserts that Dunn went to training camp with the Tigers sometime between 1910 and 1916 but hurt his arm and had to retire. This is supported by a photo of Frank Dunn in a Detroit uniform and a baseball autographed by Ty Cobb. Thus far, additional details have proved difficult to pin down.

In any event, Tom Murphy was living in Detroit at the time of the 1910 census, still unmarried, and working at the local ballpark. Before the 1911 season, he spent three weeks in Monroe, Louisiana, preparing the Tigers' spring training grounds. He returned from Monroe raving about the medicinal value of the salt water baths: "Before diving into the tepid and saline waters of the Monroe pool," the *Washington Post* reported, "Mr. Murphy says that he needed spectacles when reading the box scores, form charts, interviews with [Cubs owner] Charles Webb Murphy, or other classical literature. Now all is changed and he has thrown away the glasses. The finest print bothers him not at all, no matter how poor the light."[4] Nevertheless, Tom left Detroit within two years for parts unknown.

A "groundkeeper Murphy," identified in one newspaper as James Murphy, prepared a new Chicago ballpark for its opening in 1914, but given journalists' frequent confusion about groundskeepers' names, it is possible that this was Tom.[5] If true, it would be nice to think that fans who today enjoy the beauty of the stadium now known as Wrigley Field are savoring a plot of ground first prepared by this groundskeeping pioneer. Another note had a "Groundkeeper Murphy" working for Buffalo in 1918, and this too could have been Tom. But that is the last possible glimpse of him in the historical record, and even the members of SABR's Biographical Committee (see this book's afterword) have been unable to determine when and where Tom Murphy died.

Pat Murphy's baseball career is discussed at some length in the afterword. The details of his life after baseball are also somewhat sketchy. We know that he was an Indianapolis fireman for the last sixteen years of his life. We can assume that, if he was anything like his brothers, he was meticulous about his work. When his wife passed away in 1889, Murphy was left as the only parent of a five-year-old daughter, Bessie. Because baseball took Pat Murphy far from Indianapolis, members of his late wife's family assumed most of the responsibility for raising Bessie. The prominence of Patrick's tombstone suggests, however, that father and daughter remained close.

As discussed in the afterword, an 1892 article implied that the other two brothers, Michael and Morris Murphy Jr., also worked as groundskeepers. If so, neither was destined for a long career, or life. Michael died on November 11, 1900, and Morris Jr. on July 8, 1903.

The harrying season of 1913, during which John Murphy had to deal with the dual occupancy of the Polo Grounds, was his last. On the morning of September 19, with the Giants on the verge of clinching another pennant, Mary Agnes Murphy came home from shopping to find her husband dead. Just as his brother Patrick had two years earlier, John had succumbed to a sudden heart attack. He had been hard at work right until the end, traveling to New London, Connecticut, only a week before his death to supervise work on that city's diamond.[6]

Tributes to the veteran groundskeeper were widespread and effusive. An Associated Press wire story observed that Murphy was "known wherever the game is played as the builder and conditioner of diamonds."[7] The *Sporting News* wrote that "Murphy was undoubtedly the greatest genius in his line. Not only did his craft shine in decorative design, but he kept the playing field in perfect condition. Ball players in both leagues declare it the very best ground in the country."[8] The *Atlanta Constitution* added that Murphy was "a living encyclopedia of information about ball players and the national game."[9]

But perhaps the tribute that the veteran groundskeeper would have appreciated most was the Giants players' vote to give $1,000 of that year's World Series purse to his widow.[10]

12. The Murphys' Legacy

In the twenty or so years between the hiring of Tom Murphy to re-
shape Baltimore's Union Park and John Murphy's death in 1913, the
game had undergone extraordinary changes. In almost all of them,
the role of the "dirt beneath the fingernails" was considerable, and in
many of them the two brothers' involvement was direct. Some of these
changes have already been discussed in previous chapters, but others
took place more gradually and only in hindsight can their scope be
fully appreciated.

The Murphy brothers entered the groundskeeping profession when
even major league stadiums left much to be desired. In 1887, for example, a reporter proclaimed that the new grounds in Philadelphia
were "the most complete and best appointed" to date, even though
he also acknowledged that "no matter how hard the ball was hit it
rolled only a few feet after striking the earth."[1] By the end of the Murphys' careers, the desirability of level playing fields was accepted, and
owners had begun to give groundskeepers the manpower and the
machinery to accomplish that goal. Boston groundskeeper John Hag-
gerty observed in 1904 that "when a young player fumbles the ball he
blames the grounds, saying they are full of holes. The old fellows never
complained of grounds, simply saying they were as good for one as for
another."[2] In the decades since, level surfaces have become so universal
that they are now taken for granted even at minor league and Little
League parks.

As a result, few people today appreciate how difficult it is to make seemingly routine defensive plays on a hilly surface. The most unfortunate aspect of this loss of historical perspective is the tendency of contemporary baseball analysts to deprecate the defensive skills of nineteenth-century players. Such analysts generally make little allowance for the fact that most fielders before the mid-1880s wore no gloves or sunglasses and take equally little account of the hardships of playing on an uneven surface.

For these reasons, it's worthwhile to note the havoc wrought by the few exceptions to the level playing field since the days of the Murphys. Even after level playing fields became commonplace, hills in front of some outfield fences continued to be used to help outfielders avoid colliding with the outfield wall. As outfielders began to become accustomed to the flat surfaces at most ballparks, however, it became virtually impossible for them to adjust to these few remaining hills. In 1915, for example, sportswriter W. A. Phelon explained that "The left field embankment at the Reds' park is a very pretty little bit of landscape gardening, but a maddening obstacle to the fielders. When a ball is hit up that bank on the roll, they usually miss the rebound, and pursue it madly down the sward, while the batter goes galloping for two or three bases, and the crowd expresses itself in unhallowed phraseology. When a ball is sent up there on the fly, the fielder gives it up; simply stays down at the bottom of the bank, and waits for it to light and return to him." Phelon observed that Cincinnati outfielder Wade Killefer had recently caused "a popular consternation" by catching two balls after running up the hill.[3]

By the 1950s, these slopes leading up to the outfield wall had been removed at most ballparks. One exception was Cincinnati's Crosley Field. Visiting outfielders consequently had to make special preparations for the now unaccustomed experience of running up a slope. Ralph Kiner recalled that "the trick was to plant yourself about three steps from the incline and then when you broke back, you counted those three steps to yourself. If you didn't you'd stumble and fall everytime."[4]

The elimination of these hills had caused some frightening collisions. This resulted in the introduction in the late 1940s of warning tracks, which enabled outfielders to sense their distance from the wall by the change in surface beneath their feet. With outfields now entirely level, outfielders were increasingly instructed to watch only the course of the ball, since they could take the levelness of the ground for granted. This development has enabled outfielders to gauge balls more accurately and look more graceful. Yet few have recognized that this appearance first depended on the institution of level playing fields.

The historical point was driven home when in 2000 Houston unveiled a new ballpark that included a small hill in deep center field. The hill was the brainchild of Astros executive Tal Smith, who conceived it as a tribute to old-time ballparks. Instead, it served to vividly demonstrate just how entrenched level playing fields had become. When Houston center fielder Craig Biggio took a couple of well-publicized pratfalls on the hill, fans reacted by signing an online petition to demolish the hill.[5] Imagine how Biggio would have reacted to the "turtle backs" that used to mar the middle of baseball diamonds, let alone the trenches at Pendleton Park!

Another important example of how improvements to the grounds changed the way the game was played was the introduction of the infield fly rule before the 1894 season. What had come to be known as the "trapped ball play"—by which a fielder deliberately caught a ball on the short hop instead of on the fly in hopes of starting a double play— had been around since the 1860s. Despite its deceptiveness, there had never been enough agitation to abolish it. That changed in the 1890s, and a prime reason was that better playing surfaces were making the trapped ball play look too simple. Sportswriter John H. Gruber (the same man who we saw running the ill-fated footrace against John Murphy in chapter 7) later explained that the trapped ball was exciting as long as it had "an element of danger connected with it" because the risk that the ball would "strike a pebble or take a 'funny' bound . . . and result in both runners being safe" was considerable. But as hillocks and other obstacles were removed from playing fields, the play began

to look "so much like cold-blooded murder—the runners clearly having no chance." This in turn began to offend "the American idea of fair
play" and led to the infield fly rule.[6]

In some ways, John Murphy's specialty was the polar opposite of
his brother's. John produced level fields of breathtaking beauty while
Tom was best known for creating a field that was beautiful only to
those beholders who were rooting for the home team. Yet the accomplishments of both men made manifest the need for level, well-irri-
gated fields and underscored the considerable progress made toward
that goal.

Advances in tarpaulins, which in the nineteenth century had only
been used to cover bases and other limited areas, complemented this
progress. In 1906, a sportswriter noted that "Protection for the diamond during rain varies at different parks. Some clubowners protect
only the pitcher's slab or the home plate, others cover the bases as
well, and one clubowner, [George] Tebeau of Louisville, is said to have
a circus tent with which he covers the whole infield when it rains."[7]
Soon the search for a more practical solution commenced in earnest.
A Washington inventor named Lee Lamat announced plans in 1907 to
"build a truck on very wide wheels, which will be placed in the center
of the diamond. The canvas is rolled up on it and will be run out in all
directions covering the entire infield by means of small trucks, which
carry the canvas to the extremes of the infield. In this way the infield
can be covered and protected from the rain in less than ten minutes,
and it can be cleared and ready for play in about the same time."[8]

Appropriately, it was at Pittsburgh's Exposition Park that a full-
scale tarpaulin was first used. Before the 1908 season, the Pittsburg
Waterproof Company applied for a patent on a transportation truck
that would make it possible to cover the entire playing field with a giant tarpaulin: "The tarpaulin will contain 1,800 yards of brown paraf-
fined duck and will cost $2,000," a sportswriter noted. "It will be 120 x
120 feet square. The center of the tarpaulin will be attached to a truck
10 x 15 feet. The truck will be three feet high and the wheels will have a
tire six inches wide." This must have sounded like a dream come true

to Pirate owner Barney Dreyfuss, and he signed a contract that called for extensive use:

> Before and after a game, particularly in threatening weather, the truck will be run out and the playing ground covered with the tarpaulin. Should there be a shower within half an hour of time for beginning the game, or should there be a heavy rain at night, the tarpaulin will protect the playing field, and there should be no more deferred games on account of wet grounds, unless the rain should fall during the progress of a game. It is calculated that the cover can be spread in 15 or 20 minutes and removed within the same length of time. When not in use it will be folded on top of the truck and the latter trundled to a remote part of the field.[9]

The "canvas tent" was unveiled for the first time on May 6 and proved a success.[10]

Baseball had come a long way since the Murphys had entered the profession in the 1880s, when the best draining fields were still those that could be played on no more quickly than a few hours after a heavy rain. Contrast that delay with umpire Billy Evans's description of the groundskeeping crew's efficient response to the rainfall that interrupted a 1917 game: "man after man started coming on the field with wheelbarrow after wheelbarrow filled with top soil and sawdust. In extremely bad places gasoline was poured over the sawdust, then mixed in with the soil and ignited. Inside of 25 minutes the field was in such good shape that one would have hardly known it had rained."[11]

Another innovation that benefited groundskeepers was the outdoor batting cage. One of the earliest was introduced in 1896 by legendary University of Chicago football coach Amos Alonzo Stagg, who expected that the cage would "keep the men from tramping over the outfield until the grass, which is about to be sewn, has got a start."[12] The first portable batting cage was patented in 1907, and no doubt John Murphy was grateful for having less traffic on his grass.[13]

Yet another instance of the way groundskeepers' contributions have been taken for granted is the strip of bare ground known as the alley or pitcher's path that used to run from home plate to the pitcher's area of most early ballparks. The feature has recently been revived at stadiums like Arizona's Bank One Ballpark and Detroit's Comerica Park, but few fans have any idea of its purpose or why it disappeared. Researcher Tom Shieber has contended that the alley was originally borrowed from cricket, where it was designed to ensure a smooth hop on bowled balls. He explained that it was of use in baseball because early catchers stood back of the plate and caught pitches on the bounce.[14]

Shieber's theory makes sense, but it doesn't explain why the alleys remained long after catchers began stationing themselves directly behind the plate. The logical explanation for their persistence is that with grass being very difficult to maintain in well-trodden areas, the alleys represented the groundskeepers' best effort to limit foot traffic on the grass portion of the diamond. It was probably not easy getting the players to adhere to this, but at least the groundskeeper and his assistants themselves could do so. This would also account for why the alleys gradually disappeared without much notice being taken. As ventilation and irrigation improved and the sizes and budgets of grounds crews increased, it became less important to keep foot traffic off the grass. Eventually, the alleys began to be eliminated entirely and, as with so many other elements of the groundskeeper's craft, scant attention was paid.

When Houston's new ballpark opened in 2000, in addition to his controversial hill in deep center field, Tal Smith also suggested the installation of "an old-time strip between the mound and the plate . . . but some pitcher complained about the ball taking bad hops and the strip went out."[15] The obvious irony is that the feature was nixed in 2000 for precisely the reason it had been initiated some 140 years earlier. The underlying and unappreciated reality is clear: field conditions had improved so dramatically that grass was now considered to provide more reliable bounces than "skinned" areas.

A home team naturally becomes accustomed to the eccentricities of its field and derives an advantage from this familiarity. Until the early twentieth century, this fact didn't trouble most onlookers. As Christy Mathewson asked rhetorically in 1912: "otherwise what was the use in being home?" Yet, by then, attitudes were already changing, and unusual conditions were being addressed by ground rules. Sportswriter Joe S. Jackson described such an instance in 1911:

> At York, Pa., in the Tristate, they had a stand at one time that was almost on top of the plate. . . . The York catchers studied the angles for a little while and experimented with pitched balls. Then they were ready. With a runner on third they would signal for a wild pitch, and let it go to the stand. The runner would start home, the catcher would get the ball on the rebound, and the man would die at the plate. The trick was checked through adoption by the league of a permanent grounds rule for this park.[16]

In 1909, the American League passed a rule taking the final say about the ground rules away from the home club and leaving it up to the umpire if the two teams' captains could not reach an agreement.[17] The target of the rule was Tigers manager Hughey Jennings, the former Orioles mainstay who hired Tom Murphy later that same year. During his first two years as Detroit manager, Jennings had become "notorious for getting the best of the ground rules," in the words of sportswriter Jack Ryder.

> At big days at Bennett park the ropes are stretched in such a way as to force the overflow crowd into right field, leaving the other side of the garden open. Then Hughey Jennings establishes a ground rule to the effect that all hits into the crowd are to go for three bases. With that bunch of left-hand hitters, all of whom pull the ball toward right field, it is easy to see what a hunch the Tigers have before the game starts. [Matty] McIntyre, [Sam] Crawford, [Ty] Cobb and [Claud] Rossman have to put the ball into the right field crowd and jog around to third base, that's all.[18]

Changes such as these had a dramatic effect on home field advantages. Home teams in the major leagues in the 1870s won at a .563 clip, and this rose to .583 in the 1880s. In the 1890s, with Tom Murphy holding forth in Baltimore, the percentage hit an astonishing .603. With the renewed attention to fair play, however, the figure dropped to .552 in the first decade of the twentieth century and fell again to .540 in the 1910s. Since then, the home field advantage has largely stabilized: .543 in the 1920s; .553 in the 1930s; .544 in the 1940s; .539 in the 1950s; .541 in the 1960s; .538 in the 1970s; .541 in the 1980s; and .537 in the 1990s.[19]

Perhaps the most conspicuous change during the Murphys' years in baseball was the development of steel-and-concrete stadiums. The major league's first such park was Philadelphia's Shibe Park in 1909. As if to demonstrate that this structure completed the metaphorical transition of ballparks from "tents" to "pyramids," it was billed as a "lasting monument."[20] The next fifteen years saw the opening of eight similar ballparks and the first references to them as stadiums. Two points about these new ballparks are usually stressed—the engineering breakthroughs that made them possible and the rash of fires in wooden bleachers that made them essential. Both are undeniably important, yet they have caused an equally crucial factor to be overlooked.

In 1908, John E. Brown was the secretary of the game's governing body, the National Commission, and also a shareholder in the St. Louis Browns. That year, the Browns had an opportunity to purchase a piece of land, but took too long to do so and therefore ended up paying far more than the original price. Brown accordingly warned major league clubs that they were "going to be confronted with a serious problem within the next few years so far as well locating grounds in the big cities are [sic] concerned. It is policy right now for the clubs in the major leagues to purchase their grounds, for in a few years, it will be impossible to get grounds in large cities which can be easily reached by the cars."[21] On the face of it, this was the same warning that Henry Chadwick had issued more than forty years earlier. Yet the final word of Brown's advice inadvertently signaled what was new and critically different this time. Brown was referring to streetcars, but the advent of the automobile era had begun to represent an enormous challenge to major league baseball.

Fans were already beginning to expect space for parking, a factor that increased once again the amount of land necessary for a ballpark, and more dramatically than ever before. As a result, many existing major league ballparks were effectively obsolete or would soon become so. Yet automobiles also represented a tremendous opportunity because they enabled clubs to consider locations that would previously have been unreachable for fans.

Baseball had reached a crisis. With urban real estate prices again on the rise, purchasing land or acquiring a long-term lease was essential before building steel-and-concrete stadiums. The permanence of these new stadiums was a double-edged sword—a potential goldmine if a wise choice was made but fool's gold if the site did not allow for expansion. Moreover, the expense of both the stadiums and the land meant that owners would have only one opportunity to make the right choice and would spend years regretting a poor decision.

Quite a few owners made far-sighted selections and reaped the benefits. Ben Shibe was tipped off that the city planned to close Philadelphia's Hospital for Contagious Diseases and bought the adjacent land at a bargain rate.[22] When Shibe Park opened in 1909, it reflected the changing times by featuring "a two-hundred-car public garage equipped with a complete service department," as well as an auxiliary garage for the vehicles of management and ballplayers.[23] The crosstown Phillies took notice and revamped their own park at season's end: "The main reason for the rebuilding of the left field bleachers is to make room beneath for a garage," the *Sporting News* noted. "The Fifteenth Street side of the grounds on the outside has always been crowded and many persons have been kept away from games in the past because they did not care to risk their machines in the street. Under the new plans every machine can be taken care of and will be safe in the garage."[24]

This emphasis on parking was an important component of the

owners' message to the middle-class audience they sought to attract: we are here to stay and we share your values and ambitions. The country had finally switched from pitching tents to building homes, and baseball owners such as Charles Ebbets made a like promise to fans: "a club should provide a suitable home for its patrons. This home should be in a location that is healthy, it should be safe, and it should be convenient."[25]

The owners built this theme into their new homes in a variety of ways. For example, it was customary well into the twentieth century for visiting players to dress in their hotels and walk to the ballpark in their uniforms. This was considered a good way to create excitement about the day's game, but it could also subject the players to harassment en route to the ballpark. Just as importantly, as more fans were driving to the games, the sight of ballplayers walking to the stadium in their uniforms suggested an unseemly cheapness. On June 19, 1906, the National League passed a resolution that requested clubs to provide dressing rooms for visiting clubs. The lack of room for such facilities, however, meant that most road teams continued to dress in their hotels. Among the new wave of concrete-and-steel stadiums, clubhouses for the visiting teams became standard. With that, baseball's image received a much-needed boost.

Ben Shibe was not the only owner to respond shrewdly. White Sox owner Charles Comiskey played on grounds leased from the Chicago Cricket Club from 1900 to 1909, but the flat terrain led to recurrent drainage problems. He repeatedly said that he intended to build a permanent park as soon as he could afford to purchase grounds and build a stadium.[26] With his lease set to expire, he bought a twelve-plus-acre tract of land at Wentworth Avenue and 35th Street in January 1909 for Comiskey Park. His timing was exquisite in more ways than one, as the land had been in the family of former mayor "Long John" Wentworth for three generations and was changing hands for only the second time since the federal government granted it to the Illinois and Michigan canal commissioners in 1834.[27] Because the land had long been used as a community garbage dump, Comiskey was able to buy

the plot for the modest sum of $100,000. When work on the site be-
gan, one of the builder's first projects was to install "a modern system
of gravel subsoil and tile drainage under the entire city square which
has been purchased for the White Sox' use."[28]

When Pirates owner Barney Dreyfuss announced the location
of Forbes Field, according to historian Donald G. Lancaster, "they
laughed at him because the new area had nothing but the Schenley
Farms and a few buildings. Many did not believe the city would expand that far east, but Dreyfuss saw the location eventually growing
into Pittsburgh's cultural center."[29] As noted earlier, John Brush signed
a long-term lease for the Polo Grounds a few years later, and fortune
would also smile on his choice.

These owners had acted in the nick of time. The automobile would
transform American cities over the next two decades, and clubs in locations with limited potential for expansion would pay a stiff price.
Sportswriter John B. Sheridan observed in 1922 that "The man who
drives his car to the baseball park takes on a free-for-all fight" for the
few parking spots on the street.[30] This new reality caused many fans
to think twice about visiting a stadium that lacked its own parking
facilities. Worse, as automobiles became the symbol of middle-class
status, limited parking deterred the very fans whom baseball was eager
to attract.

Brooklyn would become the ultimate symbol of how much was at
stake. Like so many other parks, Ebbets Field was built on the site
of a longtime garbage pit. The locale was commonly referred to as
Pigstown because farmers had brought their pigs to feed there.[31]
Ebbets Field was initially very profitable, but a shortage of nearby
parking ultimately played a major role in the departure of the Dodgers.[32] Ballparks had entered a new era in which "if you build it, they
will come" no longer applied. It had given way to a new motto: "If you
build it, and provide enough parking, they will come."

Groundskeepers were also beneficiaries of baseball's new awareness
of its image. As we have already seen, John Murphy began to be treated
as a valued professional, and many of his colleagues were also accorded

new tokens of respect. It become more common, for example, to refer
to them as superintendents, and they were given assistants who took
care of the more menial duties. This improvement in their status put
groundskeepers squarely in the artisan tradition. Head groundskeepers began to apprentice their successors, resulting in the Murphys being the first of several noteworthy groundskeeping families including
the Schwabs and the Bossards. Neither John nor Tom had any children, but Tom served as a mentor to head Cardinals groundskeeper
Edward Truelieb, while John tutored Henry Fabian and Joe Hornung
among others.

The bounty presented by the new ballparks also had another important benefit for the two established major leagues: soon almost every major league team had a fireproof ballpark. With the blessing of
the owners, municipalities passed strict new building codes for ballparks. This posed an enormous financial obstacle for any rival league,
one that plagued the Federal League and deterred other leagues from
starting.[33] This new tactic of using building codes to maintain exclu-
sivity, together with the sharp drop in the home field advantage and
the other changes of the early twentieth century, had a cumulative
effect on baseball: a movement toward a new form of collective thinking on the part of ownership. Owners had long understood that the
economics of baseball were peculiar and did not always follow the
conventional logic of capitalism. Most had become successful by competing with and putting rivals out of business. The first part of this
formula—competing—applied to operating a baseball team, yet the
second one didn't, since a baseball club that puts all its rivals out of
business will have nobody to play! As obvious as the point seems now,
many clubs of the 1860s and 1870s realized too late that this was what
they had effectively done by monopolizing the talent.

Major league owners had gained some appreciation of baseball's
peculiar economics as early as 1879, when they put their heads together on the reserve clause. There was, however, little precedent to
help them decide when to act competitively and when to act coopera-
tively. This became particularly evident during the 1890s, as the game

lurched precipitously from the ultracompetitive Orioles to the equally extreme idea of the anticompetitive baseball trust.

The owners had not entirely resolved this dilemma by the time of John Murphy's death in 1913, but they had taken a number of important steps. As we discuss in the epilogue, owners had come to understand that they had to act collectively in order to create the perception that the game is being conducted on a level playing field.

Epilogue

The pride that Tom and John Murphy took in the physical manifestations of their work was evident, and they would no doubt gain some satisfaction from this book's belated acknowledgment of their craftsmanship. The Murphys would probably be puzzled by any attempt to attach symbolic importance to those labors, and yet their contributions in that less tangible realm also deserve recognition. Although undervalued in their day and entirely forgotten by ours, this seemingly unremarkable family was noteworthy also because they participated in and embodied a major strain in the American experience.

The Murphys, both in their lives and their vocations, exemplified the transience and impermanence that was engrained in the lives of many nineteenth-century Americans. The practice of setting up home and moving on was rooted in three basic realities: that virgin soil is easiest to cultivate, that rainfall and soil conditions enable any given region to sustain only specific crops, and that fields become infertile if not tended carefully. Even Americans who were aware of the implications of these facts couldn't afford to be too concerned about them. As discussed in the introduction, as long as land was abundant, wasteful practices were taken for granted. There was little reason to study seed selection, crop rotation, soil composition, and fertilizers when it was easier and more productive to just move along to another tract of virgin soil. As historian James MacGregor Burns noted of Southern agricultural practices, "Instead of crop rotation or fertilization, planters abandoned worn-out land to weeds and cleared more until it too was sterile. Overseers made few efforts to restore fertility to the soil by plowing clover or peas; instead they plowed up and down on slopes for cotton rows and cultivated them, leading to serious soil erosion."[1]

As Americans ran out of new frontiers, they were forced to adapt. In the first half of the century, most of them looked to soil improvement for the secret to remaining on a single plot of land. Instead of looking for greener pastures, Americans embraced the new challenge of trying to make the grass they already had greener. As we've noted, many of the Founding Fathers eventually turned from matters of state to practical tinkering with the soil. Additional encouragement of the emerging science of soil improvement was derived from the agricultural colleges and experiment stations that came into vogue to study scientific methods of farming. The very focus of the careers of John and Tom Murphy—baseball groundskeeping—embodies this new emphasis on learning how to keep the same plot of land fertile year after year.

Attitudes are even harder to adjust than habits, a theme well illustrated by the divergent paths of the two brothers. Some of the men who were reared with the frontier mentality remained forever stuck in that mold, while others eventually found a home. Tom Murphy thought he had found a home in Baltimore and, when he lost it through no fault of his own, he never settled down again. John Murphy took many years to find a permanent home, but finally did put down roots at the Polo Grounds. In this, as in so many other ways, the Murphys' lives mirrored the course of a generation of Americans who were running out of new frontiers and had to establish permanent bases.

Of course, the Murphys did not formally articulate their feelings on these topics, but that itself is a fact that deserves consideration. As we have seen, the Murphys were part of the large group of Americans who were most directly affected by their era's tidal wave of change yet had little opportunity to express their feelings in conventional forms. It is easy to assume that the resulting silence means consent to or at least compliance with that change, but that was not always the case. As historian Howard Zinn has noted, "The full extent of the working-class consciousness of those years—as of any years—is lost in history, but fragments remain and make us wonder how much of this always existed underneath the very practical silence of working people."[2] Some reading between the lines in other words is unavoidable.

Historian Paul E. Johnson did this splendidly in his recent study of the life of Sam Patch, a skilled craftsman who gained celebrity in the 1820s through a series of daring leaps at waterfalls. Patch's only comments about his leaps were mysterious statements such as "Some things can be done as well as others." Newspapers representing the Whig establishment were quick to dismiss Patch by parodying his slogan as "somebody besides other folks can do something."[3] Yet Johnson convincingly demonstrates that Patch's early jumps were actually made in response to specific slights he perceived against members of America's working class.[4] Johnson suggested that Patch's jumps and even his cryptic motto can be viewed as one blow in "an early round in the contest over recreational space in industrializing America, a contest that regularly pitted the noise and physicality of working-class recreation against the privatized, contemplative pursuits of the middle class."[5] Taken in context, the jumps represented a passionate defense of the dignity and rights of the working class.

Despite newspapers' efforts to obscure Sam Patch's message, the working classes understood it, and his celebrity showed that it resonated. This fact was nicely symbolized when Andrew Jackson, the first U.S. president to have risen from humble origins, named his favorite horse Sam Patch.[6] Sam Patch the craftsman described his leaps as "nothing more than an art which I have the knowledge of and courage to perform."[7] Johnson explains that the term *art* was a very significant one: "in Patch's world a man's art was his identity-defining skill," which "affirmed the worth of men who performed those tasks." Johnson adds: "it was the possession of an art that makes a man independent and useful and therefore the sovereign equal of any other man."[8]

Johnson's framework strikes me as an excellent means for understanding not only Sam Patch but also working-class American men of the nineteenth century in general. Such men had grown up in a time when American leaders such as banker Nicholas Biddle proclaimed: "The American farmer is the exclusive, absolute, uncontrolled proprietor of the soil. His tenure is not from government. The government derives its power from him."[9] Many farmers' sons had been unable to inherit this birthright, so they moved to the cities and developed new skills that similarly defined their identity, independence, and self-worth. These working-class men found that the cities were full of rich, successful men who earned their wealth from neither the soil nor a concrete skill. They were prepared to be tolerant of such men, accepting Sam Patch's dictum that "Some things can be done as well as others." Yet they maintained a wary attitude and were quick to pick up on and resent slights, particularly ones that seemed to be directed at their art. They had cause to feel this way because the rapid expansion of cities seemed irreconcilable with these men's art. As valued artisan positions gave way to far less fulfilling factory jobs, many hard-working Americans lost something very precious to them. Yet they didn't even have the satisfaction of righteous indignation because what they had lost was intangible, and its loss could only be blamed on something even more intangible—large economic forces. As a result, when a convenient scapegoat did emerge, it could become the subject of their seemingly unjustified wrath.

Such Americans were especially distrustful of the sudden dominance of the written word. Many members of the working class were illiterate, and those who could read found with dismay how easy it is for words to distort or devalue concrete objects. The Murphy brothers were not illiterate, but they were men who distrusted abstractions and wanted their handiwork to speak for them. This helps us understand John Murphy's sometimes tense relationship with Pittsburgh sportswriters, especially after the ball game and footrace that the writers mischievously misreported in 1903.

In John Murphy's later years, he developed the habit of spelling out simple messages in the grass that he had worked so hard to grow. This aptly symbolized the fact that the Murphys' life work was their message, and they were content as long as they were allowed to express themselves. When their ability to do so was threatened, they responded with a vehemence and apparent petulance that often shocked others.

After the 1910 season, St. Louis Browns vice president Ben Adkins issued a startling announcement: "[American League] President [Ban] Johnson insisted that we must select a man of integrity for manager. We want a man of integrity, but we went one point further, and insisted that he must also be of social standing. You know there have been managers who perhaps have been good in a way; but when it came to social prominence they wouldn't do at all." Sportswriter Joe S. Jackson scoffed at this, writing that the "manager of social standing will be expected to be 'at home' before and after games, receiving the directors, their friends, and others whose names are in the blue book, in a boudoir that will be fitted up in the clubhouse." Jackson suggested that such a manager would also be expected "to pour tea in the marquee that will occupy a shady corner of the lot, and into which the owners and friends will retire when wearied of walking around and chatting with the outfielders, between catches by the handsome young society men who will be employed to do the St. Louis gardening work."[10]

The humor masked a serious issue. Before the Civil War, baseball players had generally come from middle- to upper-middle-class backgrounds, but that had changed after the war. Baseball gradually became a path of upward mobility for the economically disadvantaged and for new immigrants—for everyone, in fact, except for African Americans. In the process, however, the prestige of ballplayers was damaged. By the twentieth century, baseball players were becoming famous and sometimes rich, but their social status remained dubious. The stereotype of the ballplayer was of a drunken, violent oaf with minimal education and uncouth manners. Unfortunately, too many players lived down to this stereotype and were guilty of well-chronicled misdeeds that tainted the entire profession.

Many hotelkeepers banned late-nineteenth-century baseball teams from their premises altogether. Marrying a ballplayer was an even greater no-no. Chicago outfielder Bill Lange had to agree to retire from baseball in order to marry into a socially prominent family, while minor leaguer Warren Beckwith had to elope with the granddaughter of Abraham Lincoln.[11] Chicago infielder Ned Williamson's father-in-law explained that his daughter had married the ballplayer over their protests: "My wife thought that professional ball players were just not the class of people she would like to have her daughter thrown in with, and therefore she refused to allow Nettie to meet any of the men."[12]

Baseball's owners contributed to the problem with penny-pinching tactics that undercut their efforts to appeal to middle-class fans. As discussed in chapter 12, any advertising benefits gained by having players walk to the park in their uniforms were probably outweighed by the lowly image thus created of the athletes in the public's mind. Similarly, the savings derived from such tactics as keeping sodden balls in play and billing players for laundering their uniforms were offset by the unsavory impression created by the dirty balls and uniforms.[13] How comfortable was a middle-class spectator likely to be with his son's idolization of a ballplayer forced to walk to the ballpark and play amid apparent squalor?

The competitive nature of baseball meant no simple solution was apparent to this problem. It was all very well to try to upgrade the sport's image by publicizing the exploits of refined collegians like Christy Mathewson and Eddie Collins, but doing so was easier said than done. Major league clubs competed fiercely for college players, but the ones like Mathewson and Collins who excelled were a distinct minority. Moreover, the collegians had leverage in the form of other job prospects, meaning that it cost baseball owners dearly to find out how good they were. This situation was wickedly satirized by Ring Lardner in his story "Back to Baltimore," in which a manager is informed by the team owner that she has signed a Yale graduate to a generous contract. The manager asks what position the newcomer plays and is told, "He ain't made up his mind yet. He has been busy learnin' his lessons." She adds that he is a gentleman who "will help you in more ways than just one." The manager wearily replies, "they's only one way he could help us and that is to get in there and play ball. If he can do that, I don't care if he's a gentleman or a policeman."[14] Naturally, this new player's refinement and intellect turn out to be entirely unaccompanied by baseball skills.

Gradually, however, the image of ballplayers improved. As it did, the metaphor of the level playing field took on a new dimension—now the players were expected to strive to become the social equals of the spectators they sought to attract. No small part of this effort was the product of the hard work of men like John Murphy to beautify baseball parks and thereby enhance the message that they were now the sport's permanent homes. And yet men like the Murphys who had worked their way up from humble beginnings were the last people to whom baseball wanted to draw the public's attention. This was part of a broader societal tendency to forget the contributions of landscape pioneers, including even those of architect Frederick Law Olmsted, the co-designer of Central Park.[15] With a man such as Olmsted relegated to complete obscurity, it was inevitable that baseball groundskeepers would be similarly forgotten.

The result was that the element of baseball most obvious to a child   that baseball is a bunch of adults playing in the dirt—began to be removed from the official version of baseball. Historians have joined in the process, with Steven Riess writing that the sites of early ballparks "were chosen according to the availability of cheap mass transit, rent prices, the social character of the neighborhood, and financial support from local transit interests."[16] Riess has listed almost every possible selection factor except the soil itself. An essential part of this sanitizing process was that the figurative elements of baseball overwrote the literal ones, enabling baseball to escape its origins and fans to experience baseball in new, more abstract ways.

This is best demonstrated by three ideas that began to emerge in the early twentieth century: streaks, milestones, and the Hall of Fame.[17] Though each of these concepts is now taken for granted by fans, they all contained hints of novelty and even subversion when they originated. For what each signified was that enormous importance might be attached to a commonplace event in an ordinary or even meaningless contest. Suddenly, an unexceptional occurrence such as a hit, a strikeout, or even just stepping onto the field could extend a streak or constitute a milestone. It could even provide a glimpse of that most elusive of human goals: fame and immortality. The result was that spectators and reporters had to pay attention in new ways, and baseball history began to become more than just a series of unsubstantiated and unverifiable claims that a given player or team was "the greatest ever."

This new significance placed an unprecedented emphasis on statistical accuracy. In 1910, the *Sporting News* made the following suggestion: "The next important evolution of base ball should be a bureau of records, the possibilities of which are as alluring as they are broad." It noted that one of the benefits "would be the preservation of acknowledged specific records, without which base ball has already been too long."[18] Baseball was starting to make a reality of a long-ago claim of pioneer sportswriter Henry Chadwick that statistics could reveal "that the modest but efficient worker, who has played earnestly and steadily through the season, apparently unnoticed, has come in, at the close of the race, the real victor."[19] And baseball had begun to place the extraordinary emphasis on records that the completists described in this book's afterword seek to perfect.

Sporting News's 1910 assessment of the state of baseball recordkeeping had concluded that "the preservation of base ball records . . . is at present left to private enterprise and is therefore on a more or less haphazard basis."[20] Leagues did release official statistics after the season, but these were often inaccurate. In an extreme example, Owen Wilson hit thirty-six triples in 1912—a record that still stands—and received no recognition. The reason was that a typographical error had led Napoleon Lajoie's thirteen triples in 1903 to be listed as forty-three (it has since been corrected to eleven). It was only the following spring that sportswriter Ernest Lanigan discovered that Wilson had established a new record.[21]

Because of this spotty recordkeeping shorter-term accomplishments such as streaks were the first to receive widespread acclaim. Fascination with streaks seems to have begun in the 1890s when several catchers, including Jim "Deacon" McGuire and minor leaguer Henry Cote, attracted considerable attention with long skeins in which they started every game. Catchers were an appropriate starting point. They had only recently begun to sport protective equipment, with the mask emerging in the late 1870s, the chest protector in the early 1880s, and the mitt in the late 1880s.[22] The sight of a catcher starting fifty or sixty consecutive games was thus simultaneously a remarkable feat *and one that it seemed safe to assume was unprecedented even in the absence of comprehensive records.*

It took longer for this interest to be transferred to players at other positions because of the enormous work involved in determining the record holder. Slowly but surely, however, the gaps were filled in. During the 1919 season, the streak of over 400 consecutive games of the Phillies' Fred Luderus seemed about to end when he was replaced in the starting lineup before a game. Statistician Al Munro Elias pleaded with the Philadelphia manager to get Luderus into the game, and he was eventually used as a pinch hitter. Luderus ran his streak to 533 games and was hailed as the new record holder. (The next year, however, he lost the record when someone discovered that nineteenth-century player George Pinkney had once played in 578 straight games.)[23]

Thereafter, the public and press began to take an active interest in streaks. During spring training in 1923, much attention was paid to the fact that Everett Scott had played in over 1,000 consecutive games. One writer crowed that "The odds against beating Scott's record in the future are anything you choose to name."[24] A few months later, a young player named Lou Gehrig made his major league debut.

Over the next two decades, much painstaking work was devoted to baseball's historical records. The result was that, in 1941, the press felt confident enough to herald Joe DiMaggio's fifty-six-game hitting streak as an unprecedented achievement, granting it enormous publicity. Such claims for DiMaggio's streak could not have been made with any assurance twenty years earlier.

Attention to milestones was slower to develop than streaks, and this again was the result of what *Sporting News* referred to in 1910 as the "haphazard basis" of baseball recordkeeping. Late-nineteenth-century newspapers sometimes noted milestones in the few statistical categories that were readily tracked, such as how many players had accumulated one hundred hits in a season. But records were not preserved systematically enough to track and compare career accomplishments.

One of the first career milestones to attract widespread attention appears to have been Cy Young's five hundredth win in 1910. This accomplishment was hailed by *Sporting Life* as "a unique feat requiring 21 years of continuous effort, which has no parallel in baseball annals, and may never be repeated by any pitcher now before the public, with the possible exception of the illustrious [Christy] Mathewson."[25] Young's five hundredth victory was the perfect candidate for this recognition for two reasons—five hundred was a relatively small number to tally, and Young's longevity made it reasonable to bill this feat as unprecedented without fear of contradiction. (Indeed, neither Mathewson nor any other pitcher before or since has come anywhere near five hundred victories.)

The same factors meant that emphasis on other milestones was slower to develop. Not only were they a great deal of work to compile, but since nobody knew how many previous players had attained that benchmark, the accomplishment lacked any context. Nevertheless, it is fair to say that consciousness of milestones was beginning to develop during the era of the Murphys, though it would not become a preoccupation until the development of reliable records for earlier players.

Just as important as streaks and milestones was the beginning of the concept of baseball immortality. Though the National Baseball Hall of Fame and Museum in Cooperstown, New York, did not open until 1939, the idea of a pantheon of great baseball feats had also emerged during the early twentieth century. In 1903, National League president Harry Pulliam had announced plans "to establish a base ball 'Hall of Fame' at League quarters in New York."[26] Pulliam's vision was simply for a wall of photographs rather than anything requiring formal membership selection. He began by mounting a life sized photo of 1902 batting champion Ginger Beaumont with the intention of adding a new one each year. The next year, Pulliam bought a photograph of 1903 batting champion Honus Wagner from John Murphy.[27]

The Hall of Fame idea began to fizzle, however, when Wagner declined the honor because of his disappointment over a poor performance in that year's World Series.[28] Moreover, since Wagner captured the circuit's batting title in six of the next seven years, it would have been a rather monotonous display even if he had been amenable. Nevertheless, the concept of a Hall of Fame was clearly one whose time had come, and it quickly caught on as a figure of speech denoting a great accomplishment. Pitching a no-hitter was the most common example, but players were also described as having entered the "hall of fame" for such feats as achieving two hundred hits in a season and pitching both ends of a double-header.[29] Thus, while the Hall of Fame and Museum at Cooperstown did not open until 1939, the metaphorical ground for the museum had been broken three decades earlier.[30]

The idea that anything that happened on a baseball field could be worthy of fame can also be seen as the logical culmination of a process begun two generations earlier by the Knickerbockers. By writing down their rules and the results of their matches, this club had started baseball's transition from an activity that was forgotten as soon as it was done to one that would be remembered. Other clubs had affirmed this course by carving out grounds and maintaining them for the purpose of playing what had previously been a child's game. The early-twentieth-century emergence of streaks, milestones, and halls of fame that memorialized and even immortalized accomplishments meant that baseball had achieved enough permanence to take the next step: from the literal to the figurative.

An essential part of this transition to the figurative was that groundskeepers became the invisible men of baseball. Nevertheless, it is important to remember them because it was their labor—the dirt beneath their fingernails—that enabled baseball to make two transformations of extraordinary importance. The first was the literal change from utilitarian fields to beautifully manicured ballparks. This in turn prompted the second transformation, which entailed a new way of conceptualizing baseball. Before the Civil War, baseball's supporters had depicted the game as a healthful recreation for men trapped in increasingly crowded and unsanitary cities. Competition soon changed the way the game was played, and the public began to increasingly associate the game with gambling and other vices. Its defenders scrambled for new ways to describe baseball's benefits, and men like Henry Chadwick generally opted for portraying the game as a test of character in which virtues like teamwork, dedication, and perseverance are rewarded. This sounded wonderful, but all too often baseball games were won by teams that did not conspicuously demonstrate these characteristics and simply had better athletes.

Baseball consequently began gradually to use an entirely new basis to justify its existence. As the nineteenth century waned, baseball's tireless groundskeepers and dedicated umpires enabled the game's proselytizers to evolve the novel line of reasoning—that a baseball game might not be won by the team with the most character, but it would at least be won by the most deserving team. This objective determination of merit would be assured by level playing fields and impartial umpires who merely interpreted a rule book.

This ideology was justified in a variety of ways that often made for strange bedfellows. Sportswriter George P. Scannell maintained in 1905 that baseball was more democratic than other sports because both sides got their innings. He noted that in football it was already the conventional wisdom that "offense is always the best defense." In contrast, a baseball team's offense could never prevent the other team's offense from getting an equal amount of time to respond. Scannell accordingly argued that

> A composite nation, if ever there was one, representing almost every creed, race and clime known to fame, we cannot very well help being liberal and fair-minded—al-

though it may come hard at times—and it is only reasonable to claim that our love for base ball is supreme and
universal, chiefly because the other fellows stand upon an
equal footing with their own pets, neither having a right,
a chance or an opening that their friend, the enemy, does
not share. Victory, from this aspect, is indeed sweet: for
it reflects a just code, an honorable test and a legitimate
result.[31]

A. G. Spalding, as noted earlier, similarly made much of the connection between baseball and democracy. Perhaps a few contemporaries questioned the gaps and omissions in Scannell's reasoning or
wondered whether a wealthy industrialist like Spalding had more than
a lip-service commitment to egalitarian principles. Such doubts, however, are likely to have troubled only a few Progressive Era Americans.
For most of them, the emotional appeal of linking the words *baseball*
and *democracy* was powerful enough to overcome any reservations.

Many of the men whose generation was shouldering the new century's work had heard their grandfathers talk of being pushed off the
farms by the impossibility of competing with mechanized farming or
of losing their valued status as artisans to economic forces they didn't
understand. They had seen their fathers try to run small businesses
in competition with the near-infinite resources of a trust. Such men
were more than willing to embrace anything approaching a level playing field.

A perfect example of this desire was the insistence of early-twentieth-century sportswriters on pointing out that fans came from all
levels of society.[32] Even social reformer Jane Addams enthused about
"the undoubted power of recreation to bring together all classes of a
community."[33] This emphasis may seem paradoxical at a time when
owners were simultaneously phasing out cheap seats.[34] Yet the unifor-
mity of the new higher prices seemed fair to the fans, and, if anything,
paying the higher prices increased middle-class fans' sense of belong-
ing, just as the introduction of fences had done half a century earlier.

Baseball thus began the twentieth century by cloaking itself in a new garb of fair play and democratic egalitarianism that would prove the perfect companion for the mood of the new century. Though American society was frequently plunged into turmoil by the new emphasis on equality of opportunity, baseball was—in its best moments—able to put a human face on the underlying societal issues.

It may seem a gross overstatement to imply a relationship between the literal and tangible playing fields that the Murphy brothers worked on so assiduously and the metaphorical "level playing field" created when Jackie Robinson shattered the color barrier. Nevertheless, significant progress toward that victory had been made by the Murphys and the many other Irishmen who broke down prejudice by proving their mettle on the baseball diamond.

When Ring Lardner's fictional manager said that he didn't care whether a man was "a gentleman or a policeman" as long as he could play ball, it was notable that he referred to one of the occupations most associated with the Irish. A. G. Spalding was still more explicit when he wrote: "The son of a President of the United States would as soon play ball with Patsy Flannigan as with Lawrence Lionel Livingstone, provided only that Patsy could put up the right article." Such acknowledgements were a small but significant step toward accepting that the color of a man's skin was equally irrelevant to whether he could play ball.

Moreover, even the most abstract metaphors derive their force from being rooted in literal realities. The notion that baseball exemplifies the idea of fair play did not materialize out of thin air any more than a level, finished playing field does, no matter how easy it now is to take both for granted. We are just as prone nowadays to take it for granted that "levelness" has always been perceived as a desirable state, and yet that isn't the case either. Indeed, the meaning of *level* has undergone a transition much like the one experienced by such words as *aggressiveness* and *hustling*. Until the twentieth century, the word *level* was primarily used to denote a reduction in the conditions of the fortunate rather than an improvement in those of the unfortunate. Dr. Samuel

Johnson's pioneering eighteenth-century dictionary defined a "leveller" as "one who destroys superiority; one who endeavours to bring all to the same state of equality." He illustrated the point with the example, "You are an everlasting leveller; you won't allow encouragement to extraordinary merit."

This negative connotation was reinforced by the political associations of the term. The Levellers were a mid-seventeenth-century British political movement that sought to "sett all things straight." However, the movement's enemies, led by Oliver Cromwell, claimed that the movement sought only to "destroy."[35] Those enemies were so effective at appropriating and demonizing the term that the Levellers were placed on the defensive. An official manifesto denied that they "had it in our thoughts to level men's estates." Another observer complained that "the word Leveller is a term of abuse cast upon many a person for holding forth of righteous principles." Eventually, a new movement called the True Levellers emerged.[36]

Even in the United States, a country founded on the principle that "All men are created equal," the term leveller was commonly used by conservatives to denigrate the advocates of radical change.[37] Moreover, as James MacGregor Burns reminds us, the Declaration of Independence's bold assertion of equality was not originally intended to be all that bold. Burns explains: "informed Americans had little thought that the idea of equality required collective action to help equalize the conditions of men born in poverty, ignorance, disease, malnutrition, and despair; they would have been aghast at the notion, if indeed they could even grasp it." Instead, they assumed men to be "equal only in their God-given natural rights to life, liberty, and property. It was obvious that men in fact—much less women and children—were most unequal in their conditions at birth and that they remained unequal in intellectual and physical endowment, economic status, intelligence, appearance, and social rank, though a few fought their way out of poverty to high position, and a few of the undeserving stumbled down the primrose path to inferior rank and disgrace."[38]

Great American writers expressed similar discomfort with any suggestion that "levelness" was a desirable aim. Edgar Allan Poe remarked that democracy only existed in nature among prairie dogs, and referred in 1841 to "the loud warning voice of the laws of *gradation* so visibly pervading all things in Earth and Heaven."[39] A year before, Ralph Waldo Emerson had warned: "The young adventurer finds that the relations of society, the positions of classes irk and sting him and he lends himself to each malignant party that assails what is eminent. He will one day know that this is not removable but a distinction in the nature of things."[40] And twenty-seven years later, Walt Whitman would describe democracy as "the leveler, the unyielding principle of the average." Yet Whitman also perceived that this leveling tendency acted in concert with another emerging concept—"individuality"— to form the "compensating balance-wheel of the successful working machinery of aggregate America."[41]

Perhaps it was not entirely a coincidence that Whitman was a former *Brooklyn Eagle* baseball reporter who penned these words just as baseball was making its greatest breakthrough. Noble but unsustainable ideals such as democracy based on equality and a republic of artisans were giving way to a new one in which a subtler balancing of factors ensured that the "machinery of aggregate America" would run smoothly. A key component in the mixture was the notion of a meritocracy—a hierarchy based on merit. Though America itself wasn't a meritocracy, the opportunity afforded by baseball compensated for a lot of inequities. After all, when real equality isn't available, most people will be content with the symbolic acknowledgment that there is equality of opportunity in at least one symbolic endeavor.

Baseball fulfilled that role, and the game was able to present itself as a meritocracy because of a foundation erected by many unacknowledged contributors, among them the Murphy brothers. It was the decision to equate the game with fair play and equality that would ultimately make it impossible to justify a color barrier. And Jackie Robinson's courage in turn made it easier for white Americans to finally realize how wrong it was to exclude any person from any activity of the basis of skin color.

It is therefore more than just a coincidence that the push for equality in the twentieth century was frequently cloaked in language that the Murphy brothers would have understood. Minorities and other disadvantaged groups appealed for a "level playing field" on which to gain a fair opportunity to compete. Though there continue to be great differences in the interpretation of what constitutes a societal "level playing field," the historical effectiveness of this rhetorical technique is shown by the fact that nobody in the twenty-first century even questions the desirability of the ideal of equity that underlies it.

Twenty-first-century discourse includes another curious borrowing from the language of groundskeeping. Many legal proceedings, especially depositions, routinely begin with a review of the "ground rules" to ensure that no unfair advantage is gained by either side. It had been, to borrow one final metaphor from the world of John and Tom Murphy, an uphill battle to get to that point.

Afterword

Cold Cases

Baseball is a game in which what happens right in front of our eyes can be the easiest to miss. The beauty and symmetry of the grass, the dirt, the chalk lines, and the outfield fence are the images that first catch and captivate our eyes, but we train ourselves to see them as backdrop to the action. Eventually, by focusing our eyes on the objects that move, we ignore the ones that permit the movement. This entire book is a story about what we miss by taking things for granted.

My interest in it started more prosaically, with a simple line of type in the baseball encyclopedias:

LAWRENCE PATRICK MURPHY, 1891 WASH (AA), DECEASED

To the Biographical Committee of the Society for American Baseball Research (SABR), those words represent a taunt. They imply that one of the participants in the national pastime has been neglected. Maybe it shouldn't much matter whether the ballplayer died alone in poverty in New Jersey in 1912 or in affluent old age in 1948 in San Francisco, surrounded by his grandchildren. And even if that information were available, goodness knows nobody would be likely to do anything with it.

But it isn't available, and that's exactly why it matters. That's what makes it a taunt, and worse, a taunt that seems to undermine what baseball is all about—that everyone's contributions matter, that nothing can be safely ignored. There is no such sense of accountability in a sport like football. The role of some players is to become buried in a pile of humanity, while others run to open spaces, and fame, and statistical recognition. If your neighbor tells you he was an offensive lineman in the NFL and once put a crushing block on Dick Butkus, good luck proving him wrong.

Baseball is different. If you meet someone who claims to have hit a double off Sal Maglie, you can, as Casey Stengel said, "look it up." Even before the statistical record reached its current state of exactitude, there was a belief that it should include every participant. Pioneer sportswriter Henry Chadwick wrote in 1864, "Many a dashing general player, who carries off a great deal of éclat in prominent matches, has all 'the gilt taken off the gingerbread,' as the saying is, by these matter-of-fact figures, given at the close of the season; and we are frequently surprised to find that the modest but efficient worker, who has played earnestly and steadily through the season, apparently unnoticed, has come in, at the close of the race, the real victor."[1] We don't much care about the gilt upon our gingerbread any more, but Chadwick's point remains relevant. Baseball's statistical records continue to matter to us because they symbolize the fundamental principle that everyone's contribution is important. Of course, not all of those statistical records compare to Babe Ruth's, but neither do all people have true equality in a democracy. Nevertheless, most of us will settle for symbolic recognition that all our contributions matter and are compiled with the same care.

Thus, the accomplishments of Lawrence Patrick Murphy appear in the encyclopedias in the same type size as Babe Ruth's. And when the word *deceased* appears in lieu of a date and place of death, it seems to undermine faith in baseball's fairness. It says "nobody knows," but it implies "he didn't have much of a career, so nobody cares." Like the grass and the dirt, we see these players, but we can ignore them. That is why something needs to be done about it!

At least that is the perspective of the members of the Biographical Committee, whose research appears in the various baseball encyclopedias and on many web sites, with credit acknowledged in agate type, if at all. The usefulness of this biographical data-hunting may be questioned, and even the committee members acknowledge it to be quixotic. There is, however, no gainsaying the diligence with which they gather complete birth and death information and other demographic data for each of the over fifteen thousand major league players.

The task is especially difficult for nineteenth-century players, who played before today's structured, hierarchical farm systems. Instead of progressing from step to step to the major leagues, players regularly showed up at a major league manager's doorstep and asked for a try-out. If the timing was good, he sometimes got the chance to play in a major league game and then, more often than not, was sent on his way, with only the Biographical Committee to wonder what became of him. Even worse, a roster player would occasionally be injured when no substitute was available, allowing a "local amateur" to emerge from the crowd and suddenly become a major leaguer.

Despite the obstacles they face, the SABR researchers usually get their man eventually, and the information they uncover constitutes an invaluable resource for baseball researchers. It has also proved valuable in unexpected ways. Several social scientists have taken advantage of the thoroughness of the available information on major league baseball players to study specific research questions, such as whether left-handers have shorter lives than right-handers.[2] In a number of instances, the Biographical Committee has helped acquaint people with an unknown branch of their family or brought about the erection of a tombstone for a long-forgotten ballplayer. On rare occasions, these researchers stumble on a discovery that provokes excitement beyond the narrow confines of the committee. In 2004 a front-page article in the *Wall Street Journal* hailed the discovery by committee members that William Edward White had become major league baseball's first African American in 1879.[3]

Ferreting out these details has also forced a rethinking of the conventional wisdom about the backgrounds of the earliest professional baseball players. Many early sportswriters—especially Henry Chadwick—saw themselves as proselytizers for the game and wrote about clean-living players from more affluent backgrounds, while tending to ignore those who had clawed their way up from poverty. As a result, it is usually members of the latter group who have been listed as "deceased," which seriously distorts any socioeconomic study of early ballplayers. In particular, the research of the Biographical Committee has added to our knowledge of the enormous contributions of Irish Americans to early baseball.

A perfect example was the player listed as Lawrence Patrick Murphy. Murphy was especially tantalizing to researchers because, unlike those maddening "local amateurs" who had been plucked from the stands for a moment of glory, Murphy had spent almost the entire 1891 season with Washington of the American Association. (The American Association was a major league that lasted from 1882 to 1891 and is not to be confused with the later minor league of the same name.) The following year, he had played for Buffalo and New Haven of the Eastern League, and then apparently ended his professional career with Indianapolis of the Western Association. Before joining Washington, Murphy had spent four seasons in the Western Association, the first three with St. Paul and the final one with Minneapolis. It also seemed likely that a P. L. Murphy who played for Birmingham and Nashville of the Southern Association in 1885 and Bridgeport of the Eastern League in 1886 was also the missing man.

There were some additional clues, although they compounded the confusion whether the player's name was Patrick Lawrence Murphy or Lawrence Patrick Murphy. The source of the existing listing appears to have been a note from the Washington correspondent of *Sporting Life*, who in 1891 referred to "Lawrence Patrick Murphy, our left fielder, who played in St. Paul last year."[4] The 1890 St. Paul city directory listed "Lawrence P. Murphy, ball player," rooming at the International Hotel. But just as much evidence seemed to point to the other order of his given names. There were several references to him as P. L. Murphy.[5] An 1890 note in *Sporting News* stated "P. Lawrence Murphy is himself once more."[6]

The Biographical Committee's file on Murphy also contained the usual red herrings. A Lawrence B. Murphy who managed Newark in

1887 was investigated but turned out to be a different man. In spite of the apparent abundance of information, none of it gave any indication of Murphy's hometown, which is absolutely crucial when trying to pin down a player with such a common surname. His playing career seemed to suggest that he had a connection with the Twin Cites, but nobody hailing from there seemed to match. With no firm leads on where to start looking for him, the search for Murphy had reached an impasse.

As often happens, it took only a single clue to send the search in a promising new direction. Researcher Reed Howard passed it along in the form of a note stating that Murphy came from Indianapolis. This new development moved Murphy's case off the back burner, and several researchers, including myself, then became involved. A search of Indianapolis city directories revealed a single listing in 1893 of "Patrick L. Murphy, ballplayer," living at 49 Johnson Avenue with a printer named Edward F. Nelson. The next step was to try to trace this man through the city's directories for preceding years. The following listings were found:

1882	Patrick Murphy, fireman, 134 Meek
1883	Patrick Murphy, laborer, 134 Meek
1884	Patrick L. Murphy, fireman, 146 Meek
1885	Patrick Murphy, fireman, 134 Meek

Then he disappeared for several years, until the 1890 directory included a listing for a Patrick L. Murphy, no occupation, at 500 East Georgia. Then another gap occurred, followed by the 1893 listing already mentioned. Patrick L. Murphy was absent from the 1894 directory and then returned in 1895 as a city fireman, which he continued to be listed as through 1911.

A now strong circumstantial case existed that this fireman was our missing ballplayer. He was listed in the directory as a fireman both before and after the baseball career of the Murphy we sought, he left the city directory during most of the ballplayer's career, and he then returned shortly afterward. Unfortunately, no direct evidence that the two men were one and the same offered itself. The fireman never lived at the same address listed in the 1893 directory for the ballplayer, so it was still conceivable that they were different men. The only thing to do was to investigate the fireman as thoroughly as possible and hope that at some point proof would emerge that he was our baseball player.

The first step was to find out what happened to the fireman, and that didn't take long. SABR stalwart Richard Malatzky checked the listings of Indianapolis's Crown Hill Cemetery and found that one Patrick L. Murphy was buried in Section 35, Lot 132, on October 9, 1911. Obituaries for this man established that he was the fireman but were brief and otherwise unhelpful. The *Indianapolis Morning Star* had ran a front-page piece about a Patrick Murphy who had died at city fire station number 11 of a heart attack. It reported that he was fifty-four years old, had been a city fireman for eighteen years, and had spent the last ten years at the station where he had died. The only survivor was a daughter, Mrs. Bessie Houppert. Unfortunately, baseball was not mentioned. Two brief death notices in the *Indianapolis News* didn't add much, nor did the death certificate, which meant that there remained room for doubt.[7]

Although researchers still believed they were on the brink of success, they also realized that they might remain perched on that brink for some time. Proving the case now became a painstaking matter of piecing together the lives of the ballplayer and the fireman to see if they were the same person. Researcher Bob Tholkes did some digging in the newspapers of the Twin Cities and discovered a striking woodcut of the ballplayer, along with this profile: "Patrick Lawrence Murphy, the popular center fielder, lives in Indianapolis. He is of Irish parentage, and first sprang into prominence in 1885, while playing in Birmingham and Nashville. He played with Minneapolis in 1886, his fine work attracting the attention of the St. Paul management, and he was signed for the season of 1887. He is a fine left-handed batsman, a first-class base runner, and is sure of any hit that comes in the vicinity of the middle garden. Murphy is twenty-eight years old, five feet seven and three-fourths inches, and weighs 170 pounds."[8] This tied the ballplayer's life together neatly and offered confirmation for what was already known. And yet there was still only circumstantial evidence that the fireman and the ballplayer were the same man.

Another tantalizing discovery was a 1912 column by old-time baseball man T. P. "Ted" Sullivan (the same man who had first recommended Marlin Springs as a spring training site). In it, Sullivan told of his days managing Chattanooga in 1892 and signing a player named Pat Murphy who was a well known slugger from the Western League. Sullivan noted that Murphy had played for St. Paul in 1887, as well as for Columbus, Minneapolis, and Indianapolis— all but Columbus corresponding to the missing player's known stops. The gist of Sullivan's column was that he could tell after one game that Murphy had lost his batting eye and could no longer play. Murphy, however, was not willing to admit this reality and made a different excuse after going hitless in each of his first four games. His excuse after the fourth game was so implausible that his teammates burst out laughing, forcing Murphy to finally acknowledge that his career was over. Sullivan ended the story by saying that Murphy "is now a rich contractor in railroad work near Indianapolis."[9]

Although Ted Sullivan was clearly thinking about the missing ballplayer, his description did not materially advance the investigation. The indication that Murphy had returned to Indianapolis was favorable, but that was offset by a profession that did not match the candidate's. Moreover, Sullivan was notorious for telling colorful stories that included many exaggerations and embellishments.

Researchers next sought confirmation by tracing the fireman's family, and census listings for him were easy to locate:

1870 census Indianapolis
Morris Murphy, 40, born Ireland, tar roofer
wife Bridget, 35, Ireland, keeps house
daughter Mary, 18, Ireland, at home
son Patrick, 16, Canada, telephone dispatch boy
son John, 14, Canada

daughter Johanna, 12, Canada
son Morris, 10, Canada
son Thomas, 7, Canada
daughter Bridget, 4, Indiana
son Michael, 1, Indiana[10]

1880 census 136 Meek Street, Indianapolis
Morris Murphy, 60, born Ireland, laborer
Bridget, 60, Ireland
Patrick, 26, Canada, laborer
Morris, 18, Canada, laborer
Thomas, 16, Canada, laborer
Bridget, 13, Indiana
Michael, 11, Indiana

The address in the 1880 census was next door to the one at which our fireman was later listed, and the fireman's brothers were often listed in Indianapolis city directories at this same address. But this only proved what was already known: that the fireman was the man who died in 1911. In 1890, the only year in which the Indianapolis directory listed Patrick L. Murphy as a ballplayer, he was living only with Edward F. Nelson, and research on this man uncovered no relationship to the fireman. So, maddeningly, it remained conceivable that the Indianapolis listing for "Patrick L. Murphy, ballplayer," was for a different man with the same name as our fireman.

You may have noticed that the census ages listed for several of the fireman's family members reflect the inaccuracy that was all too common on censuses. Patrick's age, however, was consistent in both censuses, and it was very troubling. If he was indeed born in 1854, he would have been thirty-six or thirty-seven when he made his major league debut. This would have been unusual, although it did fit well with Ted Sullivan's story about Murphy's declining eyesight. A little more doubt began to creep in.

The doubt increased as additional research made it clear that Murphy the ballplayer was well known in Indianapolis during his playing career. The Indianapolis correspondent to *Sporting Life*, for example, reported in 1889 that "Pat Murphy of the St. Pauls" was one of the local players who was preparing for the season.[11] Notes like this one made it more disturbing that the 1911 obituary had not mentioned baseball.

These doubts were fueled by researchers' memories of strong circumstantial cases that had turned out to be incorrect. In one notorious instance, researchers pursued a ballplayer named Frank Hengstebeck who was known to have been born in Poughkeepsie, New York, around 1860 and to have moved to Michigan. Since there were only three men by this name in the entire 1880 United States census, when a man matching these criteria was identified and traced, it seemed it had to be the ballplayer. Unfortunately, subsequent checking revealed that two of the three Frank Hengstebecks had all of these characteristics, and the one who had been found was the ballplayer's first cousin. If this could happen with a surname as unusual as Hengstebeck, then it could certainly happen with one as common as Murphy. Almost as disheartening to the committee was the possibility that they might never know for certain.

Then the crucial break finally came. A sad note in a sporting paper in late February 1889 read: "Center fielder Murphy of St. Paul lost his wife at Indianapolis a week ago. Murphy was taking her to Colorado, but she had been too ill to go further than Indianapolis."[12] Buried alongside fireman Patrick L. Murphy in Indianapolis's Crown Hill Cemetery there was indeed a Mary M. Murphy, who had been buried on February 22, 1889. It was known that Patrick's daughter Bessie had been living in the household of a cousin named William McBride on the 1910 census, and subsequent research uncovered an Indianapolis wedding record for Mary McBride and Patrick Murphy dated July 9, 1883.

This ended the search proper, and yet there was one puzzling loose end. When Murphy had joined Indianapolis in 1892, a local paper observed: "The Indianapolis team will play Patrick Murphy, a well-known outfielder, in right field from this afternoon on. . . . Murphy is one of the family of ball players living here, five brothers being em-

ployed on the diamond."[13] The census listings did show that Patrick
Murphy had four brothers, and the committee had discovered that
one of them, John, had played briefly in the minor leagues. But there
was no record of any playing career for the other three—Morris, Michael, and Thomas. If they were indeed employed on the diamond,
how could their efforts have been ignored?

The answer turned out to be deceptively simple. Patrick Murphy,
so obscure he had been listed only as "deceased," was a member of
the greatest groundskeeping family of his era. Patrick's brothers John
and Thomas had not merely been "employed on the diamond," they
had reshaped and reconfigured the game in myriad ways. And yet,
precisely because their contributions were so obvious, they had remained hidden in plain sight. Symbolic of this invisibility is the fact
that though John and Tom Murphy's careers intersected with so many
major baseball figures that they are frequently referred to in the sport's
extensive literature, virtually all of these works misidentify the two
men. Even John McGraw's widow, Blanche, offered a particularly confused portrait in her 1953 book, *The Real McGraw*. Blanche McGraw
appears to have retained a very vivid image of Tom Murphy, citing his
blue eyes and large mustache.[14] That makes it all the more puzzling
that she seems to have been entirely unaware that it was not Tom but
his brother John who tended the Polo Grounds for nearly a decade.
She also makes confusing references to the Polo Grounds groundskeeper as "an elderly, quiet married man" who eventually "grew old and
fell ill" and had to relinquish his duties.[15] Neither of these statements
is an accurate description of either brother.

John McGraw himself didn't mention either Murphy brother in
the closest thing he wrote to an autobiography (a series of syndicated
columns collected under the title *My Thirty Years in Baseball*). The
omission is noteworthy in view of their close connection. Still more
perplexing are the comments of Hugh Jennings, who had worked with
Tom Murphy as both a player and a manager: "Tom Murphy, fresh
from Ireland and speaking with a distinct brogue, was our groundkeeper and was just getting wise to the ways of base ball."[16] This of

a man who was born in Canada and grew up in Indianapolis with two older brothers who played professional baseball! Recent baseball scholars, including James H. Bready, Burt Solomon, and Charles C. Alexander, have repeated the misidentification of the two men.[17] In his biography of Christy Mathewson, Michael Hartley noted that "Groundskeeper Murphy is referred [sic] in sources variously as 'Tom' or 'John.'"[18] The point is not to criticize these historians, who cannot be blamed for relying on unreliable eyewitnesses like Hugh Jennings and Blanche McGraw and primary sources that generally refer only to "Ground keeper Murphy," but to underscore the fact that the Murphys have been baseball's invisible men. I hope this work will start to remedy that deficiency.

Almost as an afterthought, the *Sporting News*'s obituary of John Murphy added: "Murphy's brother, Patrick, who died suddenly in Indianapolis not long ago, was a member of the Washington League Club in 1886 and 1887." The years and league are incorrect, but it is still somewhat surprising that this clue had never been picked up by a biographical researcher. But if it had, the research that led to this book would never have been necessary and the story of the Murphy brothers would consequently have been overlooked. And that would have been a shame, wouldn't it?

Notes

Introduction

1. James MacGregor Burns, *The Vineyard of Liberty* (New York: Vintage, 1983), 3.

2. Burns, *The Vineyard of Liberty*, 5–8.

3. December 5, 1791, letter to Arthur Young, quoted in Steven Stoll, *Larding the Lean Earth* (New York: Hill & Wang, 2002), 34–35.

4. Stoll, *Larding the Lean Earth*, 8.

5. Some bat-and-ball games did incorporate the concept of foul territory, but they treated a foul ball as an out. The Knickerbockers' decision to consider a foul to be no play appears to have been unprecedented. See David Block, *Baseball Before We Knew It* (Lincoln: University of Nebraska Press, 2005), 58–59, for a fuller discussion.

6. George B. Kirsch, *The Creation of American Team Sports: Baseball and Cricket, 1838–72* (Urbana: University of Illinois Press, 1991), 95.

7. *New York Clipper*, April 28, 1860, quoted in Kirsch, *Creation of American Team Sports*, 96.

8. *Roll of Members and Constitution of the Germantown Cricket Club* (1867), quoted in Kirsch, *Creation of American Team Sports*, 96.

9. Kirsch, *Creation of American Team Sports*, 99.

10. *New York Clipper*, September 7, 1861, quoted in Kirsch, *Creation of American Team Sports*, 100.

11. Harry S. Truman, letter to Elizabeth Wallace of October 16, 1911, quoted in David McCullough, *Truman* (New York: Simon and Schuster, 1992), 80.

12. McCullough, *Truman*, 931.

13. Stoll, *Larding the Lean Earth*, 17.

14. Stoll, *Larding the Lean Earth*, 19.

15. *Memoirs of the Society of Virginia for Promoting Agriculture Containing Communications on Various Subjects in Husbandry and Rural Affairs*, quoted in Stoll, *Larding the Lean Earth*, 45.

16. Edmund Ruffin, quoted in Stoll, *Larding the Lean Earth*, 155.

17. "Extracts from an Address, delivered before the Greenville Agricultural Society, August 1841," quoted in Stoll, *Larding the Lean Earth*, 147.

18. Daniel J. Boorstin, *The Americans: The National Experience* (New York: Random House, 1973), 148–52.

19. David Stevenson, quoted in John R. Stilgoe, *Common Landscape of America, 1580 to 1845* (New Haven: Yale University Press, 1982), 117–18.

20. Both quoted in Larzer Ziff, *Literary Democracy: The Declaration of Cultural Independence in America* (Harmondsworth: Penguin, 1981), 42.

21. Madison, "An Address Delivered before the Agricultural Society of Albemarle, on Tuesday, May 12, 1818," quoted in Stoll, *Larding the Lean Earth*, 37–40.

22. December 5, 1791, letter to Arthur Young, quoted in Stoll, *Larding the Lean Earth*, 34–35.

23. Steven A. Riess, *Touching Base: Professional Baseball and American Culture in the Progressive Era*, rev. ed. (Urbana: University of Illinois Press, 1999), 9.

1. Invisible Men

1. William J. Ryczek, *When Johnny Came Sliding Home: The Post–Civil War Baseball Boom, 1865–1870* (Jefferson NC: McFarland, 1998), 33.

2. *Detroit Free Press*, May 16, 1887.

3. *Sporting News*, April 2, 1908.

4. Harry Wright correspondence, Wright to S. Mason Graffen, March 17, 1875, New York Public Library, Spalding Collection.

5. *Detroit Free Press*, May 16, 1887.

6. *Sporting News*, December 9, 1893.

7. *Detroit Free Press*, May 16, 1887.

8. *Sporting Life*, February 22, 1896.

9. *Cincinnati Times-Star*, September 17, 1887.

10. *Decatur Review*, June 1, 1904.

11. *Sporting Life*, April 6, 1895.

12. Charles Brian Goslow, "Fairground Days: When Worcester Was a National League City (1880–82)," *Historic Journal of Massachusetts* (summer 1991): 138–39.

13. *St. Louis Post-Dispatch*, May 7, 1889.

14. *Chicago Tribune*, April 25, 1914.

15. *Cincinnati Enquirer*, March 28, 1891; *Cincinnati Times-Star*, March 31, 1891.

16. *Cincinnati Enquirer*, May 27, 1891.

17. *Cincinnati Enquirer*, May 31 and June 2, 1891.

18. *Cincinnati Gazette*, June 8, 1891; *Cincinnati Enquirer*, June 8, 1891.

19. *Cincinnati Gazette*, June 21, 1891; *Cincinnati Times-Star*, June 22, 1891.

20. *Cincinnati Enquirer*, July 22, 1891; *Cincinnati Times-Star*, July 24, 1891.

21. *Cincinnati Enquirer*, August 6, 1891.

22. *Cincinnati Enquirer*, August 8, 1891.

23. *Indianapolis Star*, September 21, 1913. The afterword to this book contains additional information on the family's background.

24. Kerby A. Miller, *Emigrants and Exiles: Ireland and the Irish Exodus to North America* (New York: Oxford University Press, 1985), 292.

25. *The Encyclopedia of Indianapolis*, ed. David J. Bodenhamer and Robert G. Barrows, s.v. "Irish Hill" (Bloomington: Indiana University Press, 1994).

26. Howard Zinn, *A People's History of the United States: 1492 to Present*, rev. and updated ed. (New York: HarperCollins, 1995), 216.

27. Cecil Woodham-Smith, *The Great Hunger: Ireland 1845–1849* (1962; reprint, New York: Old Town Books, 1989), 19.

28. Ronald Takaki, *A Different Mirror: A History of Multicultural America* (Boston: Little, Brown, 1993), 140–43.

29. Takaki, *A Different Mirror*, 144.

30. I have found no specific proof that the Murphy brothers were Catholic, but their sister Johanna was, and it is virtually certain that they were as well.

31. Frederick Law Olmsted, *The Cotton Kingdom* (1861; reprint, New York: Random House, 1984), 70.

32. Quoted in Burns, *The Vineyard of Liberty*, 408.

33. W. E. B. DuBois, *Dusk of Dawn: An Essay toward an Autobiography of a Race Concept* (New York: Harcourt, Brace, 1940), 14.

34. Takaki, *A Different Mirror*, 157.

35. *Olney's Practical System of Modern Geography*, quoted in Michael T. Isenberg, *John L. Sullivan and His America* (Urbana: University of Illinois Press, 1994), 22.

36. In 1841, Benjamin Disraeli pronounced Ireland the most densely populated country in Europe (Woodham-Smith, *The Great Hunger*, 31).

37. See John Mack Faragher's introduction to *Rereading Frederick Jackson Turner*, ed. John Mack Faragher (New York: Henry Holt, 1994).

38. Frederick Jackson Turner, "The Significance of the Frontier," in *Rereading Frederick Jackson Turner*, ed. John Mack Faragher, 44–45 (New York: Henry Holt, 1994).

39. Historian David B. Danbom, for example, remarks, "Ranching was a business, not an opportunity for living out a romantic fantasy. Those—such as Theodore Roosevelt—who failed to recognize it for what it was were not destined to stay in it very long." David B. Danbom, *Born in the Country: A History of Rural America* (Baltimore: Johns Hopkins University Press, 1995), 142.

40. Danbom, *Born in the Country*, 133.

41. Sean Wilentz, *Chants Democratic: New York City and the Rise of the American Working Class, 1788–1850*, 20th anniversary ed. (New York: Oxford University Press, 2004), 56–109.

42. Steven J. Overman, *The Influence of the Protestant Ethic on Sport and Recreation* (Aldershot, England: Avesbury, 1997), 114–15.

43. James Bernard Cullen, ed., *The Story of the Irish in Boston* (Boston: James B. Cullen, 1889), 125.

44. *The Encyclopedia of Indianapolis*, s.v. "Irish."

45. *The Encyclopedia of Indianapolis*, s.v. "Irish."

46. Takaki, *A Different Mirror*, 162. As Daniel Boorstin explains, there was a direct connection between Ireland's rural history and the affinity of Irish Americans for machine politics. Daniel J. Boorstin, *The Americans: The Democratic Experience* (New York: Random House, 1973), 256–61.

47. Indianapolis city directories, 1880–1912; census listings.

48. Witold Rybczynski, *A Clearing in the Distance: Frederick Law Olmsted and America in the Nineteenth Century* (New York: Simon & Schuster, 2000), 175.

49. *Washington Post*, February 8, 1895.

50. Reprinted in the *Syracuse Post Standard*, August 26, 1910.

51. *Washington Post*, September 3, 1896; Jerrold Casway, *Ed Delahanty in the Emerald Age of Baseball* (South Bend IN: University of Notre Dame Press, 2004), 10.

52. Tim Murnane, *Washington Post*, April 29, 1906.

2. The Pursuit of Pleasures under Difficulties

1. Melvin L. Adelman, *A Sporting Time: New York City and the Rise of Modern Athletics, 1820–70* (Urbana: University of Illinois Press, 1986), 123, although Adelman corrected the tendency of prior historians to portray the Knickerbockers as extremely wealthy.

2. Letter of William Rankin, 1909, in Alfred H. Spink, *The National Game* (1911; reprint, Carbondale: Southern Illinois University Press, 2000), 54.

3. Harold Peterson, *The Man Who Invented Baseball* (New York: Charles Scribner's Sons, 1969), 69.

4. William Shepard, "Reminiscences of an Old-time Ball Player," in Seymour Church, *Baseball* (1902; reprint, Princeton NJ: Pyne, 1974), 38.

5. *Sporting News*, February 29, 1896.

6. Fanny Trollope, *Domestic Manners of the Americans* (London, 1832), 302.

7. Trollope, *Domestic Manners of the Americans*, 305.

8. Paul E. Johnson, *Sam Patch the Famous Jumper* (New York: Hill & Wang, 2003), 73–74.

9. Ryczek, *When Johnny Came Sliding Home*, 33, 65.

10. *Brooklyn Eagle*, October 3, 1861.

11. *Brooklyn Eagle*, October 4, 1861.

12. *Spirit of the Times*, September 22, 1855.

13. Peter Morris, *Baseball Fever: Early Baseball in Michigan* (Ann Arbor: University of Michigan Press, 2003), 96–101; also, Priscilla Astifan, "Baseball in the Nineteenth Century," *Rochester History* 52, no. 3 (summer 1990): 22.

14. *Spirit of the Times*, January 31, 1857, in *Early Innings: A Documentary History of Baseball, 1825–1908*, ed. Dean Sullivan, 22–24 (Lincoln: University of Nebraska Press, 1995).

15. Richard Fyfe, letter to Clarence Burton, Burton Collection, Detroit Public Library.

16. *Marshall Statesman*, September 11, 1861.

17. *Kalamazoo Telegraph*, December 10, 1901.

18. Henry Chadwick, ed., *Beadle's 1860 Dime Base-Ball Player* (New York: Irwin P. Beadle, 1860), 17.

19. Quoted in *Sporting Life*, March 13, 1909.

20. *Jackson Daily Citizen*, August 6, 1874; Morris, *Baseball Fever*, 297, 309.

21. James Frank, "History of Local Baseball Recalled as Fans Get Ready for Another 'Jackson Day' at Detroit," *Jackson Citizen Patriot*, July 21, 1935.

22. Edmund Redmond, "Subject of Famous Verse, 'Casey at the Bat,' Played Ball on Early Team Here," *Rochester Democrat and Chronicle*, July 24, 1927.

23. *National Chronicle*, June 12, 1869.

24. Goslow, "Fairground Days," 134, reports neighbors' complaints about cutting fences, trespassing, and obscenities.

25. Stephen Hardy, *How Boston Played: Sport, Recreation and Community 1865–1915* (Boston: Northeastern University Press, 1982), 85.

26. *The Ball Players' Chronicle*, June 27, 1867.

27. *Detroit Free Press*, January 13, 1889.

28. Marjorie Porter, *Detroit News*, August 31, 1919.

29. Federal Writers' Project, *Baseball in Old Chicago* (Chicago: A. C. McClurg, 1939), 12–13, 22.

30. *Baseball in Old Chicago*, 23.

31. *Toronto World*, February 15, 1884. Peter Levine, in *A. G. Spalding and the Rise of Baseball: The Promise of American Sport* (New York: Oxford University Press, 1985), 46, blames the federal government for forcing the club's relocation by enforcing the terms on which the land had been given to the city. He cites the *New York Clipper* of March 29, 1884, May 31, 1884, and July 5, 1884.

32. *Brooklyn Eagle*, February 24, 1884.

33. *St. Louis Post-Dispatch*, February 21, 1884.

34. Quoted in Michael Benson, *Ballparks of North America* (Jefferson NC: McFarland, 1989), 343.

35. *Chicago Times*, reprinted in *Detroit Advertiser and Tribune*, June 28, 1866.

36. Quoted in Morris, *Baseball Fever*, 141.

37. *Niles (MI) Democrat*, July 11, 1868.

38. *Adrian (MI) Times and Expositor*, October 14, 1870.

39. *Brooklyn Eagle*, August 15, 1865.

40. *Boston Globe*, January 24, 1915.

41. Louis A. Flanagan, quoted in *New York Times*, June 4, 1895.

42. *Grand Rapids Daily Eagle*, August 24, 1868; *Grand Rapids Times*, September 17, 1874.

43. Al Pratt, quoted in *Sporting News*, March 23, 1895.

44. See Peter Morris, *A Game of Inches: The Stories Behind the Innovations That Shaped Baseball* (Chicago: Ivan R. Dee, 2006), vol. 1, *The Game on the Field*, 43–47, for more details.

45. *Boston Globe*, January 24, 1915.

46. Quoted in Benson, *Ballparks of North America*, 343.

47. *Spirit of the Times*, June 13, 1868, cited in Ryczek, *When Johnny Came Sliding Home*, 33.

48. Redmond, "Subject of Famous Verse 'Casey at the Bat,' Played Ball on Early Team Here."

49. Indeed, balls hit over the outfield fence were not always home runs in early baseball.

50. William Humber, *Diamonds of the North: A Concise History of Baseball in Canada* (Toronto: Oxford University Press, 1995), 32.

51. Harry Wright correspondence, Wright to Charles Neal, January 8, 1879, New York Public Library, Spalding Collection.

52. See Morris, *A Game of Inches*, 1:491–92, for more details on blocked balls, and Peter Morris, *A Game of Inches: The Stories Behind the Innovations That Shaped Baseball* (Chicago: Ivan R. Dee, 2006), vol. 2, *The Game Behind the Scenes*, 58–59, for more on the history of ground rules.

53. Ryczek, *When Johnny Came Sliding Home*, 33.

54. *Portage Lake (Houghton MI) Mining Gazette*, August 25, 1870.

55. *Adrian Times and Expositor*, July 6, 1871.

56. Quoted in James M. DiClerico and Barry J. Pavelec, *The Jersey Game: The History of Modern Baseball from Its Birth to the Big Leagues in the Garden State* (New Brunswick NJ: Rutgers University Press, 1991), 175.

57. *New York Clipper*, September 26, 1863.

58. Spink, *The National Game*, 402.

59. *Sporting News*, June 14, 1886.

60. Tom Melchior, *Belle Plaine Baseball, 1884–1960* (self-published, 2004), 30.

61. Unidentified 1868 guide, quoted in "Quaint and Odd Things from Baseball Guides of the 60s," *Washington Post*, June 30, 1907.

62. *Winona Republican*, April 21, 1876.

63. Adrian Anson, *A Ball Player's Career* (1900; reprint, Mattituck NY: Amereon, n.d.), 19.

64. *Michigan Argus*, September 16, 1870.

65. *Ionia (MI) Sentinel*, June 25, 1875.

66. *Chicago Tribune*, June 2, 1918.

67. See Warren Goldstein, *Playing for Keeps: A History of Early Baseball* (Ithaca NY: Cornell University Press, 1989), 48–53, for a detailed discussion of the factors involved.

68. *Chicago Tribune*, March 12, 1901.

69. *New York Clipper*, January 12, 1878.

70. *Boston Globe*, October 1, 1883.

71. James Pender, *History of Benton Harbor and Tales of Village Days* (Chicago: Braun Publishing, 1915), 76.

72. Quoted in Goslow, "Fairground Days," 137.

73. *Worcester Evening Gazette*, April 22, 1880, quoted in Goslow, "Fairground Days," 137–38.

74. *St. Louis Post-Dispatch*, March 17, 1884.

75. *Worcester Evening Gazette*, May 10, 1880, quoted in Goslow, "Fairground Days," 138–39.

76. *Detroit Advertiser and Tribune*, June 23, 1865.

77. Clarence Deming, "Old Days in Baseball," *Outing*, June 1902, 358.

78. *Evart (MI) Review*, August 4, 1876.

79. *The Campion*, May 1916, reprinted in *Sporting News*, June 1, 1916.

80. *St. Louis Globe-Democrat*, March 30, 1883.

81. *Boulder News and Courier*, July 9, 1880.

82. Connie Mack, "Memories of When the Game Was Young," *Sporting Life* (monthly), June 1924.

83. See Morris, *A Game of Inches*, 1:264–73, for a more detailed summary of the history of sliding.

84. *New York Clipper*, September 3, 1881.

85. *San Francisco Examiner*, November 11, 1888.

86. *Sporting News*, June 17, 1886.

87. *Chicago Times*, reprinted in *Detroit Advertiser and Tribune*, October 20, 1866.

88. *Winona Republican*, June 9, 1876.

3. Inside Baseball

1. Burt Solomon, *Where They Ain't* (New York: Free Press, 1999), 71.

2. The term in fact was not new, but it became associated with the Orioles.

3. *Sporting News*, April 26, 1923. Hugh Jennings tells the same story in his autobiography, *Rounding Third* (n.p., 1925).

4. *Detroit Free Press*, May 16, 1887.

5. Quoted in Mrs. John J. [Blanche] McGraw, *The Real McGraw*, ed. Arthur Mann (New York: Van Rees Press, 1953), 94.

6. *Chicago Tribune*, August 5, 1906.

7. Reprinted in *The Scrapbook History of Baseball*, ed. Jordan A. Deutsch et al. (Indianapolis: Bobbs-Merrill, 1975).

8. John J. Evers and Hugh S. Fullerton, *Touching Second: The Science of Baseball* (1910; reprint, Mattituck NY: Amereon House, n.d.), 294.

9. *Chicago Tribune*, August 5, 1906.

10. Solomon, *Where They Ain't*, 77; Jack Kavanagh and Norman Macht, *Uncle Robbie* (Cleveland: SABR, 1999), 18.

11. See McGraw, *The Real McGraw*, 94; Solomon, *Where They Ain't*, 71–76; Christy Mathewson, *Pitching in a Pinch* (1912; reprint, Mattituck NY: Amereon House, n.d.), 293–95.

12. *Chicago Tribune*, August 5, 1906.

13. Harry Weldon, *St. Louis Post-Dispatch*, September 24, 1897.

14. Reuel Denney, *The Astonished Muse* (Chicago: University of Chicago Press, 1957), 108.

15. Denney, *The Astonished Muse*, 113.

16. Quoted in McGraw, *The Real McGraw*, 94.

17. Quoted in McGraw, *The Real McGraw*, 94.

18. John J. McGraw, *My Thirty Years in Baseball* (1923; reprint, Lincoln: University of Nebraska Press, 1995), 66.

19. *Sporting News*, March 23, 1895.

20. *Sporting Life*, September 19, 1896, quoted in Casway, *Ed Delahanty in the Emerald Age of Baseball*, 126. The *Chicago Tribune* of August 24, 1896, published an article that similarly claimed that the Irish were "quick-witted," which made them better ballplayers and policemen than the "phlegmatic" Germans.

21. *Washington Post*, February 25, 1907.

22. Quoted in McGraw, *The Real McGraw*, 94.

23. *Sporting Life*, May 4, 1895.

24. See Morris, *Baseball Fever*.

25. *Boston Globe*, March 28, 1897.

26. Albert Goodwill Spalding, *America's National Game: Historic Facts Concerning the Beginning, Evolution, Development, and Popularity of Base Ball, with Personal Reminiscences of Its Vicissitudes, Its Victories, and Its Votaries* (1910; reprint, Lincoln: University of Nebraska Press, 1992), 301.

27. Casway, *Ed Delahanty in the Emerald Age of Baseball*, 42–50.

28. Mathewson, *Pitching in a Pinch*, 291.

29. Spalding, *America's National Game*, 412.

30. *Washington Post*, February 17, 1897.

31. *Detroit Free Press*, July 1, 1888.

32. *Sporting Life*, May 5, 1894.

33. John Schwartz, "From One Ump to Two," *Baseball Research Journal* 30 (2001): 85–86.

34. Spalding, *America's National Game*, 302–3.

35. Spalding, *America's National Game*, 315.

36. James D. Hardy Jr., *The New York Giants Base Ball Club: The Growth of a Team and a Sport, 1870–1900* (Jefferson NC: McFarland, 1996), 105, 229.

37. Hardy, *The New York Giants Base Ball Club*, 174–75; Robert F. Burk, *Never Just a*

Game: Players, Owners and American Baseball to 1920 (Chapel Hill: University of North Carolina Press, 1994), 153.

38. Hardy, *The New York Giants Base Ball Club*, 188–89. Roosevelt announced plans to prosecute J. P. Morgan's railroad trust on February 18, 1902, in the midst of the battle over the baseball trust.

39. Hardy, *The New York Giants Base Ball Club*, 183.

40. Hardy, *The New York Giants Base Ball Club*, 188.

41. Spalding, *America's National Game*, 414–15.

42. Spalding, *America's National Game*, 6.

4. Who'll Stop the Rain?

1. *New York Sun*, September 19, 1913.

2. *Sporting Life*, July 15, 1885.

3. *Sporting Life*, September 30, 1893; *Sporting Life*, September 26, 1891.

4. *Sporting Life*, January 9, 1904.

5. Evansville is not included because it was an independent club.

6. *Minneapolis Journal*, August 21, 1891.

7. *Sporting Life*, April 30, 1892.

8. *Decatur (IL) Review*, March 18, 1906.

9. *Sporting Life*, September 30, 1893.

10. David L. Fleitz, *Cap Anson* (Jefferson NC: McFarland, 2005), 140, 192–93.

11. *Sporting Life*, June 3, 1893.

12. *Sporting Life*, December 9, 1893.

13. *Sporting Life*, October 21, 1893; *Sporting Life*, December 9, 1893.

14. *Sporting Life*, May 5, 1894.

15. *Washington Post*, February 8, 1895.

16. *Washington Post*, March 11, 1895.

17. Washington correspondent, *Sporting Life*, April 20, 1895.

18. *Sporting Life*, July 20, 1895, and September 28, 1895.

19. *Sporting Life*, November 23, 1895.

20. *Sporting Life*, December 18, 1897.

21. *New England Base Ballist*, October 29, 1868.

22. *New York Clipper*, February 19, 1870.

23. *Toronto World*, January 12, 1885.

24. Ray Schmidt, *Two-Eyed League: The Illinois-Iowa League of 1890–1892* (self-published, 1994), 87.

25. McGraw, *The Real McGraw*, 54.

26. William J. Ryczek, *Blackguards and Red Stockings* (Jefferson NC: McFarland, 1992), 180.

27. Philip Lowry, *Green Cathedrals: The Ultimate Celebration of All 271 Major League and Negro League Ballparks Past and Present* (Reading MA: Addison-Wesley, 1992), 153.

28. Greg Rhodes and John Snyder, *Redleg Journal* (Cincinnati: Road West, 2000), 70.

29. Henry Ellard, *Base Ball in Cincinnati: A History* (1907; reprint, Jefferson NC: McFarland, 2004), 169.

30. *Cincinnati Commercial Gazette*, December 7, 1883 (research by David Ball).

31. Rhodes and Snyder, *Redleg Journal*, 71.

32. *Sporting News*, March 7, 1896.

33. Rhodes and Snyder, *Redleg Journal*, 137. The Schwabs were another legendary groundskeeping family and, like the Murphys, its members were frequently confused. Rhodes and Snyder identify Matty Schwab as the club's groundskeeper in 1894 and 1900. However, Matty was born in 1879, and the Reds' groundskeeper during these years was Matty's father, John Schwab. Matty did assist his father and succeeded him in 1903, according to the *Sporting Life* of December 5, 1903. Matty's son and namesake was head groundskeeper of the Polo Grounds in the 1940s and 1950s and followed the club to San Francisco.

34. The *Sporting Life* of March 7, 1914, defined a *turtle back* as "a term applied to an elevated portion of the diamond laid out with the intention of draining the infield."

35. *Chicago Tribune*, March 24, 1907.

36. Reprinted in the *St. Louis Post-Dispatch*, March 15, 1884.

37. *Sporting Life*, March 26, 1884; *St. Louis Post-Dispatch*, May 5, 1884; *Cincinnati Enquirer*, May 12, 1884, reported by David Ball, *Nineteenth-Century Notes* (summer/fall 1995), 12.

38. Ryczek, *When Johnny Came Sliding Home*, 33.

39. *Trenton Times*, April 28, 1885.

40. *Chicago Tribune*, August 5, 1906.

41. *Boston Globe*, reprinted in *Sporting Life*, April 7, 1899.

42. *Boston Globe*, reprinted in *Sporting Life*, April 7, 1899.

43. *Sporting Life*, September 8, 1900.

44. Mathewson, *Pitching in a Pinch*, 288–89.

45. *Sporting Life*, March 21, 1903.

5. A Diamond Situated in a River Bottom

1. Dan Bonk, "A Lot of History at Three Rivers Stadium," in *Baseball in Pittsburgh*, ed. Paul Adomites and Dennis DeValeria (Cleveland: SABR, 1995), 57.

2. Bonk, "A Lot of History at Three Rivers Stadium," 50.

3. A. R. Cratty, *Sporting Life*, January 9, 1904.

4. *Chicago Tribune*, May 27, 1900. In 1890 the U.S. Board on Geographic Names decreed that the *h* be dropped from the names of all cities and towns ending in *-burgh*. Many in Pittsburgh ignored the ruling, but the city's official name remained Pittsburg until 1911. For consistency's sake, I have referred to it as "Pittsburgh" throughout but have left references to it as they appeared in the original.

5. *New York Times*, September 19, 1913.

6. *Sporting Life*, August 17, 1901.

7. *Sporting Life*, December 28, 1901.

8. *Sporting Life*, January 11, 1902.

9. *Sporting Life*, March 8, 1902.

10. *Sporting Life*, March 29 and April 5, 1902.

11. *Sporting Life*, January 9, 1904.

12. *Sporting Life*, June 14, 1902.

6. Tom Murphy's Crime

1. *Sporting Life*, December 11, 1897.

2. Lowry, *Green Cathedrals*, 100.

3. Solomon, *Where They Ain't*, 118.

4. *Brooklyn Eagle*, May 10, 1899.
5. Solomon, *Where They Ain't*, 87.
6. *Sporting Life*, April 7, 1900.
7. Charles C. Alexander, *John McGraw* (New York: Viking, 1988), 68–69.
8. Alexander, *John McGraw*, 69.
9. Alexander, *John McGraw*, 68–69.
10. Riess, *Touching Base*, 63.
11. *Sporting Life*, June 15 and 22, 1901.
12. *Sporting Life*, August 9, 1902, and February 27, 1903.
13. *Sporting Life*, August 24, 1901.
14. *Sporting Life*, September 14, 1901.
15. *Sporting Life*, August 9 and 16, 1902.
16. *Sporting Life*, August 9, 1902.
17. *Sporting Life*, August 9 and 16, and September 20, 1902.

7. Return to Exposition Park

1. *Sporting Life*, April 26, 1902.
2. *Sporting Life*, May 31, 1902.
3. *Sporting Life*, April 26, 1902.
4. *Sporting Life*, April 26, 1902.
5. *Washington Post*, May 19, 1902.
6. Solomon, *Where They Ain't*, 227–30.
7. James H. Bready, *The Home Team*, cited in Solomon, *Where They Ain't*, 230. Solomon identified the perpetrator as Tom Murphy, but this is impossible as Tom was on the run from the law at the time.
8. *Washington Post*, July 25, 1902.
9. *Sporting Life*, September 20, 1902.
10. *Sporting Life*, May 9, 1903.
11. A. R. Cratty, *Sporting Life*, June 20, 1903.
12. *Brooklyn Eagle*, July 5, 1902.
13. *Sporting Life*, June 20, 1903.
14. Dennis DeValeria and Jeanne Burke DeValeria, *Honus Wagner: A Biography* (New York: Henry Holt, 1996), 136.
15. *Sporting Life*, October 31, 1903.
16. *Sporting Life*, December 5, 1903.
17. *Sporting Life*, September 12, 1903.
18. *Sporting Life*, January 9, 1904.
19. Alexander, *John McGraw*, 104, 113–15, 262.
20. A. R. Cratty, *Sporting Life*, April 22, 1905.
21. *Sporting Life*, March 7, 1914.
22. *Chicago Tribune*, May 2, 1909.
23. Bonk, "A Lot of History at Three Rivers Stadium," 59.

8. No Suitable Ground on the Island

1. Ryczek, *When Johnny Came Sliding Home*, 31.
2. Ryczek, *When Johnny Came Sliding Home*, 34.
3. Unidentified 1868 guide, quoted in "Quaint and Odd Things from Baseball Guides of the 60s," *Washington Post*, June 30, 1907.

4. *Brooklyn Eagle*, July 16, 1873.

5. *Philadelphia Sunday Mercury*, August 9, 1868, quoted in Kirsch, *Creation of American Team Sports*, 235.

6. *New York Clipper*, March 25, 1871, quoted in Kirsch, *Creation of American Team Sports*, 251–52.

7. *New York Clipper*, February 12, 1881.

8. *Brooklyn Eagle*, November 8, 1885.

9. *New York Clipper*, February 12, 1881.

10. *Brooklyn Eagle*, November 8, 1885.

11. Lowry, *Green Cathedrals*, 189.

12. Jerry Lansche, *Glory Fades Away: The Nineteenth-Century World Series Rediscovered* (Dallas: Taylor Publishing, 1991), 40.

13. Stew Thornley, *Land of the Giants: New York's Polo Grounds* (Philadelphia: Temple University Press, 2000), 19.

14. *Brooklyn Eagle*, March 2, 1884.

15. *Brooklyn Eagle*, August 9, 1884; also *Brooklyn Eagle*, August 20, 23, and 24, and September 3, 1884.

16. "Home Nines Victorious: The Allegheny Club Meets Defeat on the New Grounds," *The World*, May 14, 1884; quoted in Thornley, *Land of the Giants*, 20.

17. *Brooklyn Eagle*, February 24, 1884.

18. *Brooklyn Eagle*, November 2, 1884.

19. *Brooklyn Eagle*, February 24, 1884.

20. *Brooklyn Eagle*, March 16, 1884.

21. *National Police Gazette*, April 19, 1884.

22. *National Police Gazette*, June 21, 1884.

23. Larry Lupo, *When the Mets Played Baseball on Staten Island* (New York: Vantage Press, 2001), 13–16.

24. David Nemec, *The Beer and Whisky League* (New York: Lyons & Burford, 1994), 110.

25. *Sporting News*, May 17, 1886.

26. *New York Times*, July 10 and 15, 1888.

27. *New York Times*, April 20 and 21, 1889.

28. *New York Times*, April 9, 1889.

29. *New York Times*, February 9, 1889.

30. Tim Murnane, "Murnane's Baseball," *Boston Globe*, November 9, 1902.

31. *New York Times*, April 24, 1889.

32. *New York Times*, April 4, 1889.

33. *New York Times*, February 9, 1889.

34. *New York Times*, April 4 and 9, 1889.

35. *New York Times*, April 17, 1889.

36. *New York Times*, April 30, 1889.

37. *Brooklyn Eagle*, May 15 and 17, 1889.

38. Hardy, *The New York Giants Base Ball Club*, 86.

39. *New York Times*, May 22, 1889; Hardy, *The New York Giants Base Ball Club*, 85.

40. Thornley, *Land of the Giants*, 3.

41. *Sporting Life*, May 1, 1889.

42. *Sporting News*, November 30, 1933.

43. Thornley, *Land of the Giants*, 44.

44. *New York Times*, April 8, 1889.

45. *New York Times*, July 9, 1889.

46. It had always been assumed that polo had never been played there until researcher Peter Mancuso found a note in the May 6, 1885, issue of *Sporting Life* that read, "A new polo and baseball ground is being laid out in New York City bounded by One-Hundred and Fifty-fifth and One-Hundred and Fifty-ninth Streets and Eighth Avenue."

47. *Boston Globe*, May 10, 1890.

48. *New York Sun*, May 13, 1890.

49. *Boston Globe*, May 10, 1890.

50. *New York Sun*, May 17, 1890.

51. *St. Louis Post-Dispatch*, November 8, 1901; Riess, *Touching Base*, 73.

52. *St. Louis Post-Dispatch*, November 8, 1901.

53. Tim Murnane, "Murnane's Baseball," *Boston Globe*, November 9, 1902. "Three old cat" was one of the simple bat-and-ball games that was popular before the Knickerbockers helped to established standard rules.

54. *Washington Post*, February 26, 1906.

55. Mike Sowell, *July 2, 1903: The Mysterious Death of Hall-of-Famer Big Ed Delahanty* (New York: Macmillan, 1992), 205. The club also had to overcome the opposition of local property owners (Riess, *Touching Base*, 109–10).

56. Lowry, *Green Cathedrals*, 194.

57. *New York Times*, October 26, 1912, February 21, 1913, and June 21, 1914; Riess, *Touching Base*, 127.

58. *New York Times*, March 19, 1912.

59. *Washington Post*, June 28, 1903.

60. *Sporting Life*, April 29, 1905.

61. *Sporting Life*, February 18, 1905. Regarding the ball club's profits, the *Washington Post* of September 24, 1904, reported that the club had turned a profit of $150,000 that year. Riess provides additional details in *Touching Base*, 76–77.

9. John Murphy of the Polo Grounds

1. *Sporting Life*, February 18, 1905.

2. *New York Times*, December 21, 1912.

3. *Washington Post*, August 3, 1913.

4. *Sporting Life*, December 14, 1912.

5. *Sporting News*, September 25, 1913.

6. *New York Sun*, September 19, 1913.

7. Sam Crane, reprinted in the *Syracuse Post Standard*, August 26, 1910.

8. I. E. Sanborn, *Chicago Tribune*, September 14, 1913.

9. Harry Dix Cole, *Sporting Life*, December 14, 1912.

10. Lowry, *Green Cathedrals*, 193.

11. Sam Crane, reprinted in the *Syracuse Post Standard*, August 26, 1910.

12. Fred Lieb, *Baseball As I Have Known It* (New York: Grosset & Dunlap, 1977), 21.

13. *New York Sun*, May 17, 1912.

14. *Sporting Life*, March 4, 1905.

15. I. E. Sanborn, *Chicago Tribune*, September 14, 1913.

16. *Sporting Life*, March 24, 1906.

17. *Atlanta Constitution*, September 19, 1913.

18. *St. Louis Post-Dispatch*, September 20 and 25, 1913.

19. *New York Times*, September 19, 1913.

20. Sam Crane, reprinted in the *Syracuse Post Standard*, August 26, 1910.

21. *Bridgeport (CT) Telegram*, December 30, 1920. The exact year in which this took place was not specified, but Murphy did visit New London only a week before his death according to the *Indianapolis Star* of September 21, 1913. It would be fitting if this were his last project.

22. *Sporting News*, September 22, 1910.

23. Sam Crane, reprinted in the *Syracuse Post Standard*, August 26, 1910.

24. Rhodes and Snyder, *Redleg Journal*, 111. Rhodes and Snyder again identify the groundskeeper in question as Matty Schwab, but as Matty was only fourteen at the time it was certainly his father John Schwab.

25. Evers and Fullerton, *Touching Second*, 117.

26. Burk, *Never Just a Game*, 194, 197.

27. Evers and Fullerton, *Touching Second*, 148.

28. *Pittsburg Gazette*, reprinted in *Sporting Life*, June 23, 1906.

29. Joseph Durso, *The Days of Mr. McGraw* (Englewood Cliffs NJ: Prentice-Hall, 1969), 223.

30. I. E. Sanborn, *Chicago Tribune*, September 14, 1913.

31. *Sporting News*, July 2, 1942.

32. *Brooklyn Eagle*, August 8, 1901.

33. *New York Times*, August 26, 1901.

34. *New York Times*, October 11, 1903.

35. *New York Herald*, April 15, 1911.

36. *New York Times*, June 29, 1911.

37. I. E. Sanborn, *Chicago Tribune*, September 14, 1913.

38. *Sporting Life*, December 12, 1908.

39. *Coshocton (OH) Morning Tribune*, November 19, 1911.

40. I. E. Sanborn, *Chicago Tribune*, September 14, 1913.

41. *Sporting News*, February 15, 1934; George Ross, *Frederick (MD) Post*, October 31, 1936.

10. Marlin Springs

1. *Sporting News*, reprinted in *Chicago Tribune*, February 7, 1904.

2. Kevin Saldana, chair of the SABR Spring Training Committee.

3. *New York Times*, December 22, 1907.

4. Sam Crane, *New York Evening Journal*, February 20, 1908, reprinted in G. H. Fleming, *The Unforgettable Season* (New York: Holt, Rinehart and Winston, 1981), 19.

5. *Sporting News*, September 22, 1910; *New York Times*, December 23, 1910.

6. *New York Times*, December 21, 1912.

7. For the 1871 Mutuals, see *Sporting Life*, March 31, 1906.

8. *New York Clipper*, January 24, 1880.

9. *Brooklyn Eagle*, March 11, 1896.

10. Joe S. Jackson, *Detroit Free Press*, March 21, 1909.

11. *Sporting News*, November 19, 1898, cited in Casway, *Ed Delahanty in the Emerald Age of Baseball*, 37.

12. *Detroit Free Press*, March 3, 1909.

13. *Sporting Life*, January 28, 1905.

14. *Detroit Free Press*, March 20, 1909.

15. *Sporting Life*, March 25, 1899.

16. *Sporting Life*, March 9, 1912.

17. *New York Sun*, September 19, 1913.

18. *Sporting News*, December 8, 1910.

19. Evers and Fullerton, *Touching Second*, 223.

20. Kevin Saldana, chair of the SABR Spring Training Committee.

21. *Chicago Tribune*, February 26, 1911; *Sporting Life*, March 11, 1911.

11. The Later Years

1. *Sporting Life*, April 29, 1905.

2. *Sporting Life*, March 10, 1906.

3. *Elyria (OH) Reporter*, April 6, 1906.

4. *Washington Post*, January 21, 1911.

5. *Indianapolis Star*, February 13, 1914.

6. *Indianapolis Star*, September 21, 1913.

7. *Newark (OH) Advocate*, September 18, 1913.

8. *Sporting News*, September 25, 1913.

9. *Atlanta Constitution*, September 19, 1913.

10. *Atlanta Constitution*, October 13, 1913.

12. The Murphys' Legacy

1. *Washington Post*, May 1, 1887.

2. Tim Murnane's column, *Boston Globe*, March 20, 1904.

3. *Sporting News*, July 1, 1915.

4. Quoted in David Falkner, *Nine Sides of the Diamond* (New York: Times Books, 1990), 186.

5. Michael Serazio, "Center of Gravity? Tal's Hill at Minute Maid Takes on an Uprising," *Houston Press* (online version), July 8, 2004.

6. John H. Gruber, "You're Out," *Sporting News*, February 17, 1916.

7. *Chicago Tribune*, September 30, 1906.

8. *Washington Post*, June 15, 1907.

9. *Sporting Life*, May 2, 1908.

10. *Chicago Tribune*, May 7, 1908. See Morris, *A Game of Inches*, 2:61–63, for more details on the history of the tarpaulin.

11. Billy Evans, syndicated column, *Indianapolis Star*, March 24, 1918. Evans noted that this energy occurred when the unnamed home team was down by a run but that during a rain delay on the day before with the home team ahead, the groundskeeper "had stalled around with about 20 men assisting and accomplished little or nothing."

12. *Decatur Review*, April 7, 1896.

13. Ken Tillman, "The Portable Batting Cage," *Baseball Research Journal* 28 (1999): 23–26.

14. Tom Shieber, presentation at SABR conference no. 35, Cincinnati, Ohio, July 18, 2004.

15. Leigh Montville, "Field of Screams," *Sports Illustrated*, May 22, 2000.

16. *Washington Post*, March 24, 1911.

17. *Detroit Free Press*, February 18, 1909.

18. Jack Ryder, quoted in *Detroit Free Press*, February 4, 1909.

19. Bill James, *The New Bill James Historical Baseball Abstract* (New York: Free Press, 2001), 13, 39, 57, 75, 98, 125, 148, 200, 224, 252, 279, 298, 312.

20. Souvenir program, quoted in Bruce Kuklick, *To Every Thing a Season: Shibe Park and Urban Philadelphia, 1909–1976* (Princeton NJ: Princeton University Press, 1991), 25. A. G. Spalding, ever alert for a good marketing tool, used the same phrase in *America's National Game*, 497.

21. *Sporting Life*, July 4, 1908, quoted in David W. Anderson, *More Than Merkle* (Lincoln: University of Nebraska Press, 2000), xx.

22. Kuklick, *To Every Thing a Season*, 24.

23. Kuklick, *To Every Thing a Season*, 28.

24. *Sporting News*, December 9, 1909.

25. Quoted in Riess, *Touching Base*, 99.

26. George W. Hilton, "Comiskey Park," *Baseball Historical Review* (1981): 1.

27. "In Real Estate Circles," *Chicago Tribune*, January 24, 1909, H18.

28. "Work Is Started on New Sox Park," *Chicago Tribune*, May 11, 1909.

29. Donald G. Lancaster, "Forbes Field Praised as a Gem When It Opened," *Baseball Research Journal* 15 (1986), 26.

30. *Sporting News*, February 9, 1922.

31. Michael Gershman, *Diamonds: The Evolution of the Ballpark* (Boston: Houghton Mifflin, 1993), 110.

32. Riess, *Touching Base*, 79, 124 27; Neil J. Sullivan, *The Dodgers Move West* (New York: Oxford University Press, 1987), 38–41.

33. Riess, *Touching Base*, 121.

Epilogue

1. Burns, *The Vineyard of Liberty*, 286.

2. Zinn, *A People's History of the United States*, 216.

3. *New England Palladium*, quoted in Johnson, *Sam Patch the Famous Jumper*, 91.

4. Patch's first jump occurred after the 1828 Independence Day celebrations in Paterson, New Jersey, in which a number of slights had been directed at working-class men, such as excluding them from their usual place in the parade. His second leap was similarly made during a dispute about hours at the mill where he worked. See Johnson, *Sam Patch the Famous Jumper*, 61–71.

5. Johnson, *Sam Patch the Famous Jumper*, 51.

6. Johnson, *Sam Patch the Famous Jumper*, 180–81.

7. Quoted in Johnson, *Sam Patch the Famous Jumper*, 53.

8. Johnson, *Sam Patch the Famous Jumper*, 53 54.

9. "An American Farmer," *Niles' Weekly Register*, October 22, 1936, quoted in Andrew Burstein, *Sentimental Democracy: The Evolution of America's Romantic Self-Image* (New York: Hill & Wang, 1999), 330. Biddle in turn echoes de Crevecoeur's rhetorical question, "where is that station which can confer a more substantial system of felicity than that of an American farmer, possessing freedom of action, freedom of thoughts, ruled by a government which requires but little from us?" Hector St. John de Crevecoeur, *Letters*

from an American Farmer (London: J. M. Dent & Sons, 1912), 56. See Danbom's *Born in the Country*, 66–67, for additional examples.

10. *Washington Post*, December 23, 1910.

11. And, as Lawrence S. Ritter chronicled in *The Glory of Their Times* (1966; reprint, New York: William Morrow, 1984), 38–39, early-twentieth-century player Davy Jones gave up his high school sweetheart when forced to choose between her and baseball (although they met and married many years later, after both had been widowed).

12. *Boston Globe*, March 11, 1894.

13. The members of the White Sox/Black Sox were notoriously said to have "had to pay for having their uniforms laundered and it got to be such an expense they wore them dirty rather than pay. Then, when they left town, the Sox management went through their lockers, laundered all the dirty uniforms, and 'docked' the amount from their salaries" (*Chicago Tribune*, July 12, 1921). But they were far from unique.

14. Ring Lardner, "Back to Baltimore," in *The Annotated Baseball Stories of Ring W. Lardner, 1914–1919*, ed. George Hilton (Stanford: Stanford University Press, 1995), 431.

15. Rybczynski, *A Clearing in the Distance*, 418–20.

16. Riess, *Touching Base*, 132.

17. For more details, see Morris, *A Game of Inches*, 2:170–71 on streaks, 2:168–70 on milestones, and 2:348–49 on halls of fame.

18. *Sporting News*, August 18, 1910.

19. *1864 Beadle's Base Ball Guide*, 59–60.

20. *Sporting News*, August 18, 1910.

21. *Sporting News*, March 13, 1913.

22. See Morris, *A Game of Inches*, 1:421–26 for mitts, 1:432–36 for masks, and 1:436–38 for chest protectors.

23. Joe Dittmar, "Fred Luderus," in *Deadball Stars of the National League*, ed. Tom Simon (Washington DC: Brassey's, 2004), 206.

24. *Sporting News*, March 22, 1923.

25. *Sporting Life*, July 30, 1910, reprinted in Reed Browning, *Cy Young: A Baseball Life* (Amherst: University of Massachusetts Press, 2000), 188.

26. *Sporting Life*, March 21, 1903.

27. *Sporting Life*, March 26, 1904.

28. *Sporting Life*, April 2, 1904.

29. *Sporting News*, August 18, 1910; *Sporting Life*, August 30, 1913; *Washington Post*, September 10, 1911.

30. For more details on the opening of the Baseball Hall of Fame and Museum in Cooperstown, see James A. Vlasich, *A Legend for the Legendary* (Bowling Green OH: Bowling Green State University Popular Press, 1990).

31. *Sporting Life*, March 25, 1905.

32. Riess, *Touching Base*, 28.

33. Jane Addams, *The Spirit of Youth and the City Streets* (1909), quoted in Riess, *Touching Base*, 28.

34. Riess, *Touching Base*, 41–43.

35. Samuel Johnson, *A Dictionary of the English Language* (London, 1755), s.v. "leveler."

36. Christopher Hill, *The World Turned Upside Down* (Harmondsworth: Penguin, 1975), 107–23.

37. Burns, *The Vineyard of Liberty*, 60, 109, 341. A few did try to change the word's negative connotations. Sean Wilentz, for instance, notes that Mike Walsh, one of the first prominent Irish American politicians and the leader of the "shirtless" Democrats, was accused of being a leveler and responded that he "gloried in the name" (Wilentz, *Chants Democratic*, 331).

38. Burns, *The Vineyard of Liberty*, 142.

39. Edgar Allan Poe, "Mellonta Tauta" and "The Colloquy of Mono and Unas," both quoted in Ziff, *Literary Democracy*, 72 73.

40. Ralph Waldo Emerson, "Tendencies," lecture given February 12, 1840, in *The Early Lectures of Ralph Waldo Emerson*, vol. 3: 1838–1842, ed. Robert E. Spiller and Wallace E. Williams (Cambridge MA: Harvard University Press, 1972), 304–5.

41. Walt Whitman, "Democratic Vistas" (1867), in *Leaves of Grass and Selected Prose*, ed. Sculley Bradley (New York: Holt, Rinehart and Winston, 1949), 514.

Afterword

1. *1864 Beadle's Base Ball Guide*, 59–60.

2. S. Coren and D. F. Halpern, "Left-Handedness: A Marker for Decreased Survival Fitness," *Psychological Bulletin* 109: 90–106; S. Coren and D. F. Halpern, "A Replay of the Baseball Data," *Perceptual and Motor Skills* 76 (1993): 403–6.

3. Stefan Fatsis, "Mystery of Baseball: Was William White Game's First Black?" *Wall Street Journal*, January 30, 2004, 1.

4. *Sporting Life*, July 4, 1891.

5. *Columbus Evening Dispatch*, April 16, 1890.

6. *Sporting News*, May 17, 1890.

7. *Indianapolis Morning Star*, October 10, 1911; *Indianapolis News*, October 10 and 11, 1911.

8. *St. Paul and Minneapolis Pioneer Press*, March 11, 1888.

9. T. P. Sullivan, "Stories of the Diamond, *Sporting News*, March 21, 1912. This article appeared five months after Pat Murphy's death, but that fact is not significant because it was very likely a reprint that had originally appeared before Murphy's death.

10. Intriguingly, another Bridget Murphy emigrated from Ireland during this period, married another Irish immigrant named Patrick Kennedy, and became the matriarch of the Kennedy dynasty that produced a president, attorney general, and senator. Like the Murphys, they named their first two daughters Mary and Johanna and their first two sons John and Patrick. The names are so common that the families are probably not related, but it is still a striking coincidence.

11. *Sporting Life*, March 20, 1889.

12. *Sporting Life*, February 27, 1889.

13. *Indianapolis News*, June 28, 1892.

14. McGraw, *The Real McGraw*, 94.

15. McGraw, *The Real McGraw*, 187, 231.

16. Jennings, *Rounding Third*, chapter 74.

17. James H. Bready, *Baseball in Baltimore: The First Hundred Years* (Baltimore: Johns Hopkins University Press, 1998), 86.

18. Michael Hartley, *Christy Mathewson: A Biography* (Jefferson NC: McFarland, 2004), 176.

Selected Bibliography

Since groundskeepers have always been baseball's invisible men, most of the debts I have incurred in researching this book are to the authors of contemporaneous articles in local newspapers and the sporting press. Those works are cited in the notes, as are a few of the books from which I culled a useful fact or quotation. The following is a list of lengthier, retrospective works that substantively deepened my understanding of the world of the Murphys and that the reader may also find of value.

Adelman, Melvin L. *A Sporting Time: New York City and the Rise of Modern Athletics, 1820–70.* Urbana: University of Illinois Press, 1986.

Alexander, Charles C. *John McGraw.* New York: Viking, 1988.

Anderson, David W. *More than Merkle.* Lincoln: University of Nebraska Press, 2000.

Astifan, Priscilla. "Baseball in the Nineteenth Century." *Rochester History* 52, no. 3 (summer 1990): 3–23.

———. "Baseball in the Nineteenth Century, Part 2." *Rochester History* 62, no. 2 (spring 2000): 3–23.

———. "Baseball in the Nineteenth Century, Part 3: The Dawn of Acknowledged Professionalism and Its Impact on Rochester Baseball." *Rochester History* 63, no. 1, (winter 2001): 3–22.

———. "Rochester's Last Two Seasons of Amateur Baseball: Baseball in the Nineteenth Century, Part 4." *Rochester History* 63, no. 2 (spring 2001): 3–23.

———. "Baseball in the Nineteenth Century Part 5: 1877—Rochester's First Year of Professional Baseball." *Rochester History* 64, no. 4 (fall 2002): 3–23.

Benson, Michael. *Ballparks of North America.* Jefferson NC: McFarland, 1989.

Block, David. *Baseball Before We Knew It.* Lincoln: University of Nebraska Press, 2005.

Bodenhamer, David J., and Robert G. Barrows, eds. *The Encyclopedia of Indianapolis.* Bloomington: Indiana University Press, 1994.

Bonk, Dan. "A Lot of History at Three Rivers Stadium." In *Baseball in Pittsburgh,* edited by Paul Adomites and Dennis DeValeria, 57–59. Cleveland OH: SABR, 1995.

Boorstin, Daniel J. *The Americans: The Democratic Experience.* New York: Random House, 1973.

———. *The Americans: The National Experience.* New York: Random House, 1965.

Bready, James H. *Baseball in Baltimore: The First Hundred Years.* Baltimore: Johns Hopkins University Press, 1998.

Browning, Reed. *Cy Young: A Baseball Life.* Amherst: University of Massachusetts Press, 2000.

Burk, Robert F. *Never Just a Game: Players, Owners and American Baseball to 1920.* Chapel Hill: University of North Carolina Press, 1994.

Burns, James MacGregor. *The Vineyard of Liberty.* New York: Vintage, 1983.

Burstein, Andrew. *Sentimental Democracy: The Evolution of America's Romantic Self-Image.* New York: Hill & Wang, 1999.

Caillault, Jean-Pierre. *A Tale of Four Cities.* Jefferson NC: McFarland, 2003.

Casway, Jerrold. *Ed Delahanty in the Emerald Age of Baseball.* South Bend IN: University of Notre Dame Press, 2004.

Chadwick, Henry. *The American Game of Base Ball: How to Learn it, How to Play it, and How to Teach it. With Sketches of Noted Players.* 1868. Reprint, Columbia sc: Camden House, 1983. Also known as *The Game of Base Ball.*

Danbom, David B. *Born in the Country: A History of Rural America.* Baltimore: Johns Hopkins University Press, 1995.

Daniels, Roger. *Coming to America: A History of Immigration and Ethnicity in American Life.* 2nd ed. New York: HarperCollins, 2002.

Deming, Clarence. "Old Days in Baseball." *Outing*, June 1902, 357–60.

Denney, Reuel. *The Astonished Muse.* Chicago: University of Chicago Press, 1957.

DeValeria, Dennis, and Jeanne Burke DeValeria. *Honus Wagner: A Biography.* New York: Henry Holt, 1996.

DiClerico, James M., and Barry J. Pavelec. *The Jersey Game: The History of Modern Baseball from Its Birth to the Big Leagues in the Garden State.* New Brunswick NJ: Rutgers University Press, 1991.

Durso, Joseph. *The Days of Mr. McGraw.* Englewood Cliffs NJ: Prentice-Hall, 1969.

Ellard, Henry. *Base Ball in Cincinnati: A History.* 1907. Reprint, Jefferson NC: McFarland, 2004.

Evers, John J., and Hugh S. Fullerton. *Touching Second. The Science of Baseball.* 1910. Reprint, Mattituck NY: Amereon House, n.d.

Falkner, David. *Nine Sides of the Diamond.* New York: Times Books, 1990.

Faragher, John Mack, ed. *Rereading Frederick Jackson Turner.* New York: Henry Holt, 1994.

Fatsis, Stefan. "Mystery of Baseball: Was William White Game's First Black?" *Wall Street Journal*, January 30, 2004, 1.

Fleitz, David L. *Cap Anson.* Jefferson NC: McFarland, 2005.

Fleming, G. H. *The Unforgettable Season.* New York: Holt, Rinehart and Winston, 1981.

Frank, James. "History of Local Baseball Recalled as Fans Get Ready for Another 'Jackson Day' at Detroit." *Jackson Citizen Patriot,* July 21, 1935.

Gershman, Michael. *Diamonds: The Evolution of the Ballpark.* Boston: Houghton Mifflin, 1993.

Glazier, Michael, ed. *The Encyclopedia of the Irish in America.* South Bend IN: University of Notre Dame Press, 1999.

Goldstein, Warren. *Playing for Keeps: A History of Early Baseball.* Ithaca NY: Cornell University Press, 1989.

Goslow, Charles Brian. "Fairground Days: When Worcester Was a National League City: 1880–82." *Historic Journal of Massachusetts* (summer 1991): 133–54.

Hardy, James, Jr. *The New York Giants Base Ball Club: The Growth of a Team and a Sport, 1870–1900.* Jefferson NC: McFarland, 1996.

Hardy, Stephen. *How Boston Played: Sport, Recreation and Community 1865–1915.* Boston: Northeastern University Press, 1982.

Hartley, Michael. *Christy Mathewson: A Biography.* Jefferson NC: McFarland, 2004.

Hill, Christopher. *The World Turned Upside Down.* Harmondsworth: Penguin, 1975.

Hilton, George W. "Comiskey Park." *Baseball Historical Review* (1981): 1–7.

Humber, William. *Diamonds of the North: A Concise History of Baseball in Canada.* Toronto: Oxford University Press, 1995.

Isenberg, Michael T. *John L. Sullivan and His America.* Urbana: University of Illinois Press, 1994.

James, Bill. *The New Bill James Historical Baseball Abstract.* New York: Free Press, 2001.

Jennings, Hugh. *Rounding Third.* N.p., 1925.

Johnson, Paul E. *Sam Patch the Famous Jumper.* New York: Hill & Wang, 2003.

Kirsch, George B. *The Creation of American Team Sports: Baseball and Cricket, 1838–72.* Urbana: University of Illinois Press, 1991.

Kuklick, Bruce. *To Every Thing a Season: Shibe Park and Urban Philadelphia, 1909–1976.* Princeton NJ: Princeton University Press, 1991.

Lancaster, Donald G. "Forbes Field Praised as a Gem When It Opened." *Baseball Research Journal* 15 (1986): 26–29.

Lansche, Jerry. *Glory Fades Away: The Nineteenth-Century World Series Rediscovered.* Dallas: Taylor Publishing, 1991.

Levine, Peter. A. G. *Spalding and the Rise of Baseball: The Promise of American Sport.* New York: Oxford University Press, 1985.

Lieb, Fred. *Baseball As I Have Known It.* New York: Grosset & Dunlap, 1977.

Light, Jonathan Fraser. *The Cultural Encyclopedia of Baseball.* Jefferson NC: McFarland, 1997.

Lowry, Philip J. *Green Cathedrals: The Ultimate Celebration of All 271 Major League and Negro League Ballparks Past and Present.* Reading MA: Addison-Wesley, 1992.

Lupo, Larry. *When the Mets Played Baseball on Staten Island.* New York: Vantage Press, 2001

Mack, Connie. "Memories of When the Game Was Young." *Sporting Life* (monthly), June 1924, 1–3, 40, 42–43

Maier, Thomas. *The Kennedys: America's Emerald Kings.* New York: Basic Books, 2003.

Mathewson, Christy. *Pitching in a Pinch.* 1912. Reprint, Mattituck NY: Amereon House, n.d.

McCullough, David. *Truman.* New York: Simon and Schuster, 1992.

McGraw, John J. *My Thirty Years in Baseball.* 1923. Reprint, Lincoln: University of Nebraska Press, 1995.

McGraw, Mrs. John J. [Blanche]. *The Real McGraw*, edited by Arthur Mann. New York: Van Rees Press, 1953.

Melchior, Tom. *Belle Plaine Baseball, 1884–1960.* Self-published, 2004.

Miller, Kerby A. *Emigrants and Exiles: Ireland and the Irish Exodus to North America.* New York: Oxford University Press, 1985.

Moreland, George L. *Balldom.* 1914. Reprint, St. Louis: Horton Publishing, 1989.

Morris, Peter. *Baseball Fever: Early Baseball in Michigan.* Ann Arbor: University of Michigan Press, 2003.

———. *A Game of Inches: The Stories Behind the Innovations That*

Shaped Baseball. Vol. 1, *The Game on the Field*. Chicago: Ivan R. Dee, 2006.

———. *A Game of Inches: The Stories Behind the Innovations That Shaped Baseball*. Vol. 2, *The Game Behind the Scenes*. Chicago: Ivan R. Dee, 2006.

Okkonen, Marc. *Baseball Memories, 1900–1909*. New York: Sterling, 1992.

———. *The Cobb Scrapbook*. New York: Sterling, 2001.

Olmsted, Frederick Law. *A Journey in the Seaboard Slave States*. 1856. Reprint, New York: Capricorn, 1959.

Overman, Steven J. *The Influence of the Protestant Ethic on Sport and Recreation*. Aldershot, England: Avesbury, 1997.

Pender, James. *History of Benton Harbor and Tales of Village Days*. Chicago: Braun Publishing, 1915.

Peterson, Harold. *The Man Who Invented Baseball*. New York: Charles Scribner's Sons, 1969.

Redmond, Edmund. "Subject of Famous Verse, 'Casey at the Bat,' Played Ball on Early Team Here." *Rochester Democrat and Chronicle*, July 24, 1927.

Rhodes, Greg, and John Snyder. *Redleg Journal*. Cincinnati: Road West, 2000.

Riess, Steven A. *Touching Base: Professional Baseball and American Culture in the Progressive Era*. Rev. ed. Urbana: University of Illinois Press, 1999.

Ritter, Lawrence S. *The Glory of Their Times*. 1966. Reprint, New York: William Morrow, 1984.

Rybczynski, Witold. *A Clearing in the Distance: Frederick Law Olmsted and America in the Nineteenth Century*. New York: Simon & Schuster, 2000.

Ryczek, William J. *When Johnny Came Sliding Home: The Post–Civil War Baseball Boom, 1865–1870*. Jefferson NC: McFarland, 1998.

Schmidt, Ray. *Two-Eyed League: The Illinois-Iowa League of 1890–1892*. Self-published, 1994.

Schwartz, John. "From One Ump to Two." *Baseball Research Journal* 30 (2001): 85–86.

Seymour, Harold. *Baseball: The Early Years.* New York: Oxford University Press, 1960.

Simon, Tom, ed. *Deadball Stars of the National League.* Washington DC: Brassey's, 2004.

Smith, Red. *Red Smith on Baseball.* Chicago: Ivan R. Dee, 2000.

Solomon, Burt. *Where They Ain't.* New York: Free Press, 1999.

Sowell, Mike. *July 2, 1903: The Mysterious Death of Hall-of-Famer Big Ed Delahanty.* New York: Macmillan, 1992.

Spalding, Albert Goodwill. *America's National Game: Historic Facts Concerning the Beginning, Evolution, Development, and Popularity of Base Ball, with Personal Reminiscences of Its Vicissitudes, Its Victories, and Its Votaries.* 1910. Reprint, Lincoln: University of Nebraska Press, 1992.

Spink, Alfred H. *The National Game.* 1911. Reprint, Carbondale: Southern Illinois University Press, 2000.

Stark, Benton. *The Year They Called Off the World Series: A True Story.* Garden City Park NY: Avery, 1991.

Stilgoe, John R. *Common Landscape of America, 1580 to 1845.* New Haven: Yale University Press, 1982.

Stoll, Steven. *Larding the Lean Earth.* New York: Hill & Wang, 2002.

Sullivan, Dean, ed. *Early Innings: A Documentary History of Baseball, 1825–1908.* Lincoln: University of Nebraska Press, 1995.

Sullivan, Neil J. *The Dodgers Move West.* New York: Oxford University Press, 1987.

Takaki, Ronald. *A Different Mirror: A History of Multicultural America.* Boston: Little, Brown, 1993.

Thornley, Stew. *Land of the Giants: New York's Polo Grounds.* Philadelphia: Temple University Press, 2000.

Tillman, Ken. "The Portable Batting Cage." *Baseball Research Journal* 28 (1999): 23–26.

Trollope, Fanny. *Domestic Manners of the Americans.* London, 1832.

Wilentz, Sean. *Chants Democratic: New York City and the Rise of the*

American Working Class, 1788–1850. 20th anniversary ed. New York: Oxford University Press, 2004.

Woodham-Smith, Cecil. *The Great Hunger : Ireland 1845–1849*. 1962. Reprint, New York: Old Town Books, 1989.

Ziff, Larzer. *Literary Democracy: The Declaration of Cultural Independence in America*. Harmondsworth: Penguin, 1981.

Zinn, Howard. *A People's History of the United States: 1492 to Present*. Rev. and updated ed. New York: HarperCollins, 1995.

Index